bottoms

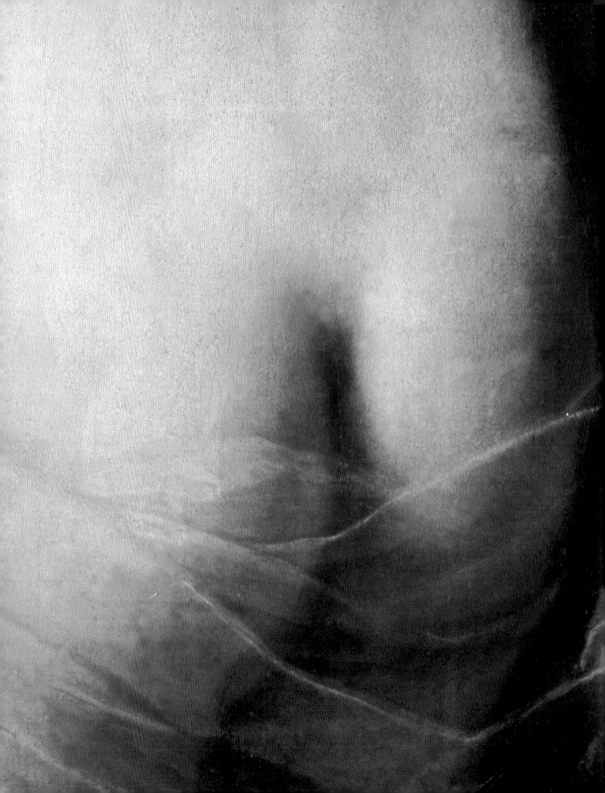

bottoms

Edward Lucie~Smith

BARNES & NOBLE
BOOKS
NEW YORK

This edition published by Barnes & Noble, Inc.,
by arrangement with
THE IVY PRESS LIMITED

2000 BARNES & NOBLE BOOKS

M 10 9 8 7 6 5 4 3 2 1

ISBN: 0-7607-2346-X

This book was conceived, designed, and produced by
THE IVY PRESS
The Old Candlemakers, West Street, Lewes
East Sussex BN7 2NZ

ART DIRECTOR Peter Bridgewater
EDITORIAL DIRECTOR Sophie Collins
DESIGNER Clare Barber
DTP DESIGNER Richard Constable
SENIOR PROJECT EDITOR Rowan Davies
CAPTION WRITER Viv Croot
EDITOR Mandy Greenfield
PICTURE RESEARCHER Liz Eddison

Printed in Singapore by Star Standard Industries (PTE) Ltd.

contents

BATHYLLVS

bare essentials...

ONE OF THE THINGS WE HAVE BEEN TRAINED OUT OF, IN THE NEW AGE OF **political correctness**, IS THE HABIT OF READING SOME OF THE WORLD'S GREAT ART MASTERPIECES IN THE WAY THEIR MAKERS INTENDED THEM—THAT IS, **SEXUALLY**. THE PARADOX IS THAT NEW ART TRIUMPHANTLY RETAINS ITS POWER TO SHOCK. INDEED, SHOCKING—OR, AT THE VERY LEAST, DISCONCERTING—THE AUDIENCE OFTEN SEEMS TO BE ITS PRIMARY PURPOSE, TRANSCENDING ANY ATTEMPT AT *esthetic appeal*. EVEN TODAY, WHEN AN ARTIST SETS OUT TO **SHOCK**, THE USE OF SEXUAL IMAGERY IS HIS OR HER MOST RELIABLE TOOL.

It often seems as if all those erotic masterpieces that hang tranquilly on the walls of so many of the world's great art galleries, and throng historic collections of sculpture, have been endowed with draperies and fig leaves not so much in fact, as in the minds of their beholders. This—so the reasoning runs—is a masterpiece by Titian, or Rembrandt, or Rubens, and therefore even the most squeamish and those who are most ready to take offense may look at it without the least disturbance to either their sense of good taste or their moral principles. Contemplation of these images can only serve to elevate the mind.

This collection of pictures has a distinctly subversive purpose. It is designed as a diversion for those moments, which happen in all our lives, when we are perhaps somewhat weary of being high-minded. To be blunt, the reaction it aims to elicit is a snigger—but (dare one say it?) a thoughtful snigger. Its subject is the human bottom. For better or worse, this feature of human anatomy has always been a subject for robust humor. It has a starring role in the innocently vulgar imagery associated with old-fashioned British seaside resorts, especially seaside postcards. And it features in stories about old-fashioned practical jokes—for instance, the large cocktail party from which the host is deliberately absent, so the guests are forced to perform the introductions themselves. It turns out that everyone is called Botham, or Winterbottom, or Shufflebottom.

Almost every image here is a detail from a celebrated work of art, a masterpiece of one sort or another. And every image represents a backside—male, female, or

BATHYLLUS POSTURING
Aubrey Beardsley (1872–98)
Engraving
1896

(just occasionally) androgynous. How many of these images can you recognize, without going to the back of the book, where the complete work is reproduced?

If you recognize a high proportion of them, what might this say about your character? That you are a frequent museum visitor? That you look at a lot of art books? That you have a retentive visual memory? Or that, in addition to some or all of these, you have an incorrigibly dirty mind?

One of the fascinating things about the cult of the bottom is that it is so ancient. The Paleolithic Venus of Willendorf has enormous buttocks, as well as large pendulous breasts. The two anatomical features are related. This is evidently a representation of a fertility goddess, and her breasts are symbolic of her power to nourish. Her plump buttocks, on the other hand, with their store of surplus fat, are symbolic of her power to survive.

The Ancient Greeks, during the sixth and fifth centuries B.C., paid rather more attention to male backsides than they did to female ones. The Archaic kouroi, the figures of beautiful youths with which the Greeks adorned their temple precincts, are magnificently equipped in this respect. The same is true of the young athletes depicted on Greek vases, whose powerful thighs and buttocks were perceived as an attribute of virility. Curiously enough, all these

LESBIAN LOVERS
Katsushika Hokusai (1760–1849)
Color woodblock print
1821

young men (both in three dimensions and in two) have somewhat undersized genitalia.

In the fourth century B.C., with the advent of the Greek sculptor Praxiteles, the emphasis was transferred from the male to the female nude. Praxiteles' Aphrodite of Cnidos set the tone for representations of nude females until the end of Greek and Roman civilization. Aphrodite is shown surprised at her bath, and as she bends forward slightly to protect her modesty, the emphasis is inevitably placed on her buttocks, which are thrust slightly backward. Less inhibited, and less tasteful, artists of the Hellenistic period were quick to take the hint. The result was the creation of the so-called Venus Kallipygos, now preserved in a number of Roman copies, where the arrangement of the figure's drapery deliberately reveals and emphasizes the curves of her buttocks.

The centuries that followed the eclipse of the old pagan world were not good ones for those obsessed with backsides, whether male or female. Artists started to feature this part of the human anatomy again only with the coming of the Renaissance. At first it tended to be male rather than female examples that predominated. There are some fine specimens to be found among the drawings of Leonardo da Vinci (1452–1519) and Michelangelo (1475–1564)—perhaps not surprisingly, since both artists were homosexual. It was, however, the painters of the Venetian School who most vigorously popularized the theme. The kind of voluptuous, fleshy female nude depicted by Titian (c. 1488–1576) in his later paintings became a favorite motif among the artists of the Baroque period. The female nudes of Rubens (1577–1640) were an unashamed celebration of fleshly abundance. He did, however, paint nude male flesh with almost equal enthusiasm. And in some instances, when depicting youthful male figures, such as Ganymede, he assimilated male and female characteristics to the point where his subject seemed to have features taken from both genders.

The artistic heyday of the backside in the postclassical epoch was, however, undoubtedly the eighteenth century. The erotic literature of the period is saturated with references to it, and its attractions play a leading role in the interminable writings of the Marquis de Sade (1740–1815). Much of the work of François Boucher (1703–70) is also—though in a lighter vein—a hymn to the attractions of this portion of the female anatomy. Boucher occupied the position of Premier Peintre du Roi (First Painter to the King), and a taste for female bottoms seems to have been something he shared with his royal master, Louis XV (1710–74). One particularly striking composition, which exists in several versions,

HERCULES AND ANTAEUS
Hans Baldung Grien (c. 1476–1545)
Oil on pine wood
1530

shows a youthful female nude sprawled prone on a bed. According to tradition, it depicts a young Irish girl named Miss O'Morphy, an inhabitant of the Parc aux Cerfs, a private brothel set up for the king's pleasure.

A curious feature of Boucher's work is that he often feminizes the male figure, to an even greater degree than Rubens. One of the tricks he employs is to give his amorous youths bottoms as plump and juicy as those of their female counterparts.

The erotic tradition founded by Titian survived throughout the nineteenth century—one of its most enthusiastic adherents, for example, was Gustave Courbet (1819–77), whose monumental *Les Baigneuses* is one of the most forthright celebrations of the female backside in art. Even after Courbet, the Impressionists and Postimpressionists retained their enthusiasm for the subject. Meanwhile in Japan the artists who celebrated the "Floating World" of the geisha or professional courtesan often featured alluring glimpses of the female backside in their *shunga* or erotic prints.

During the twentieth century both the Surrealists and the adherents of Pop continued to make use of one of the oldest, if not the most respectable, themes in art, often focusing on male buttocks. And, in an age of political correctness, this emphasis is perhaps less controversial than a celebration of the female body.

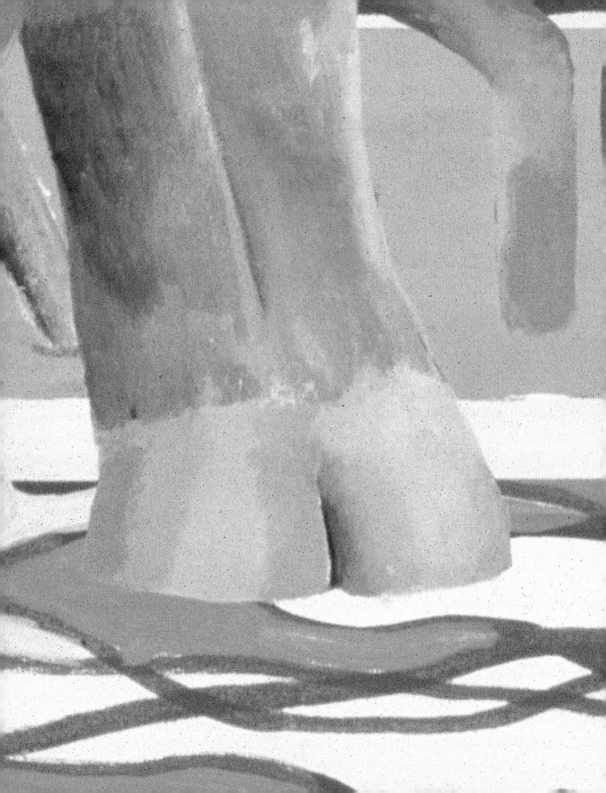

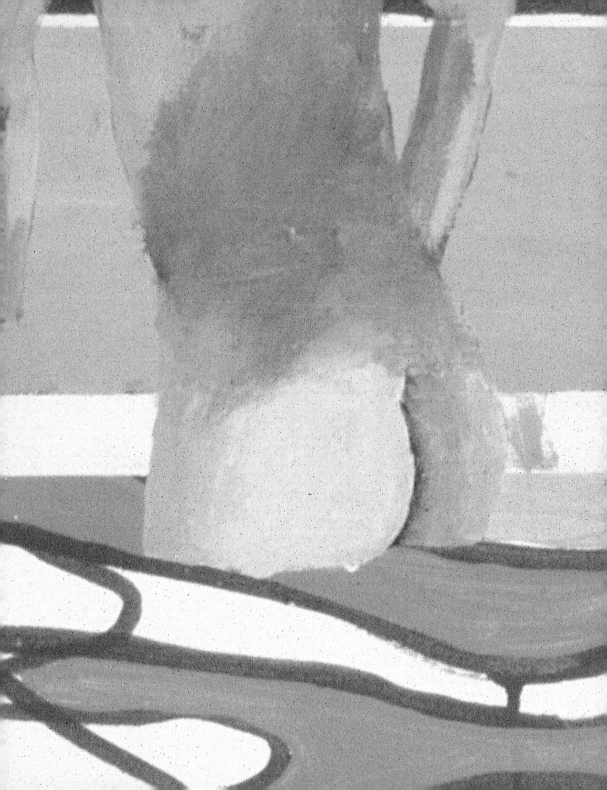

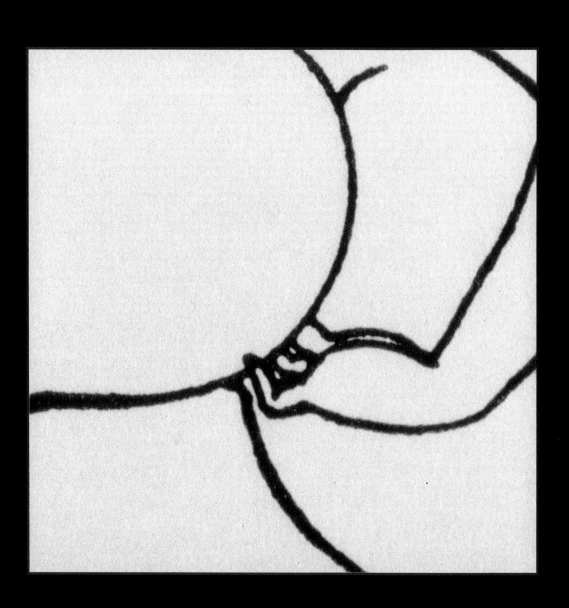

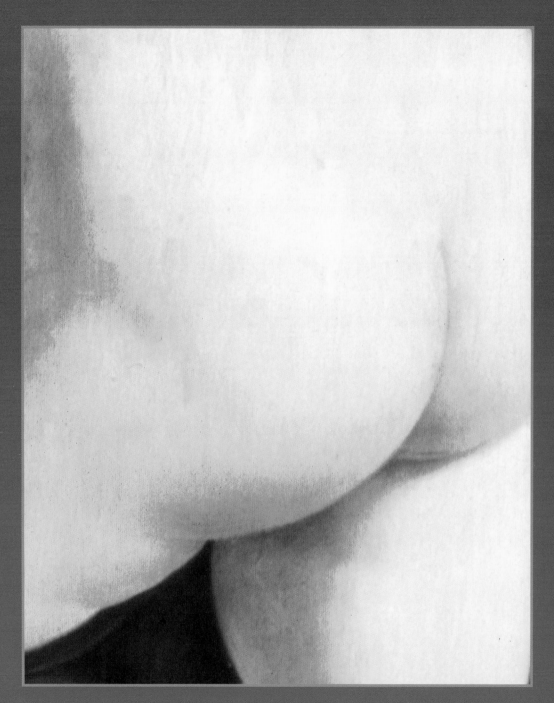

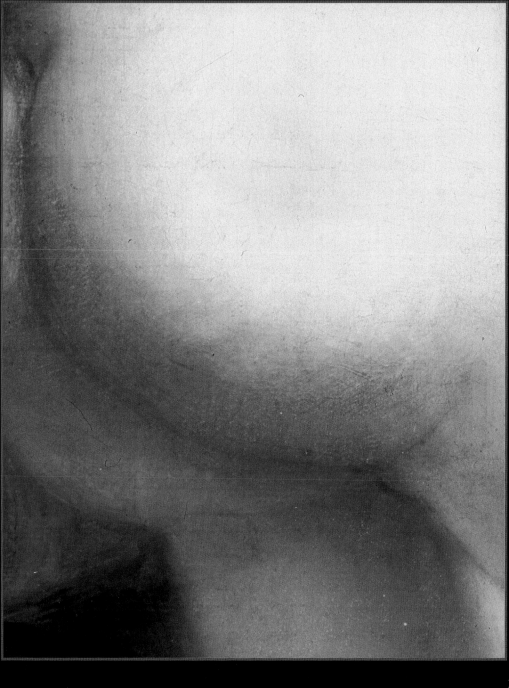

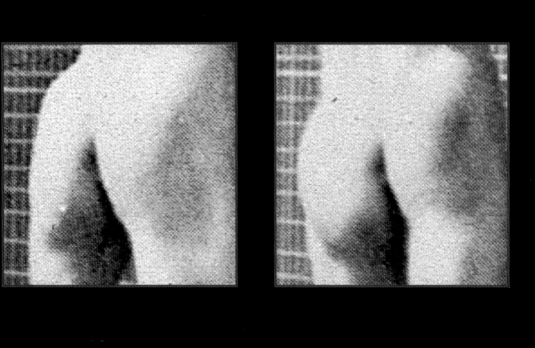

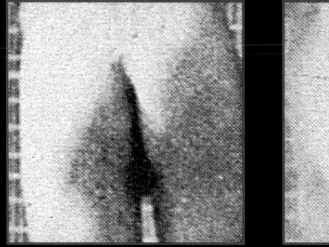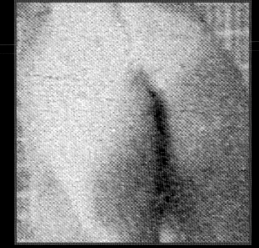

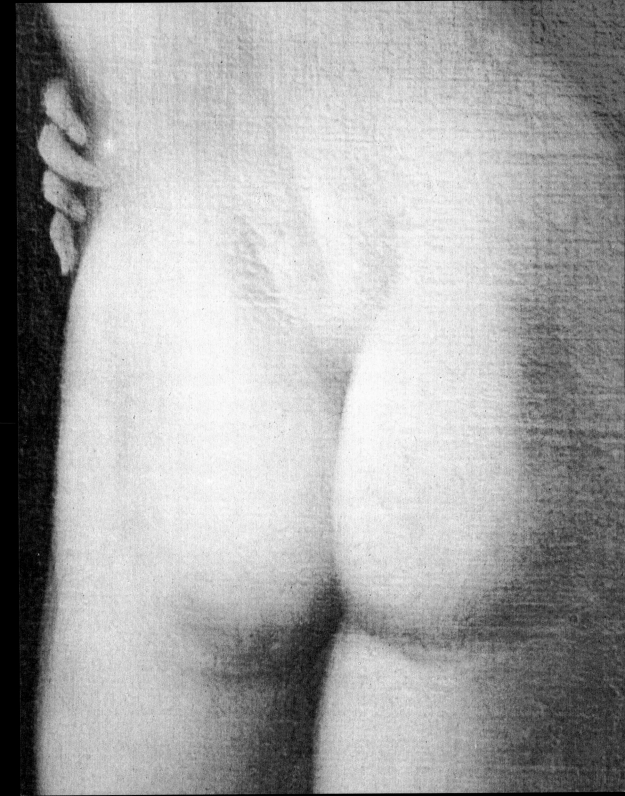

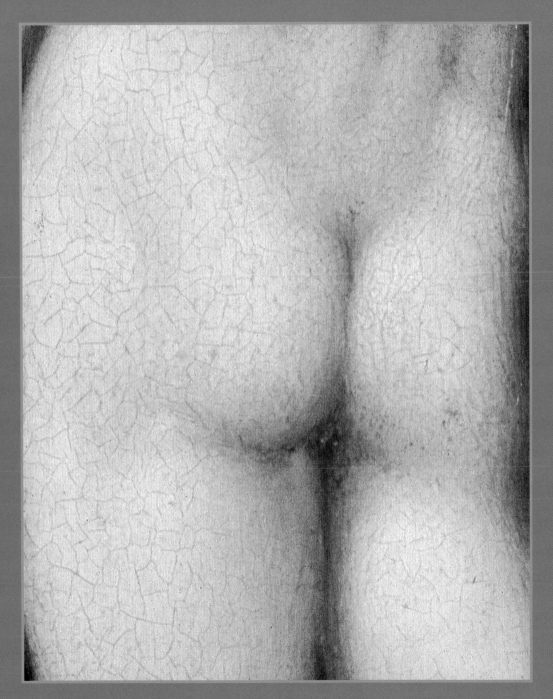

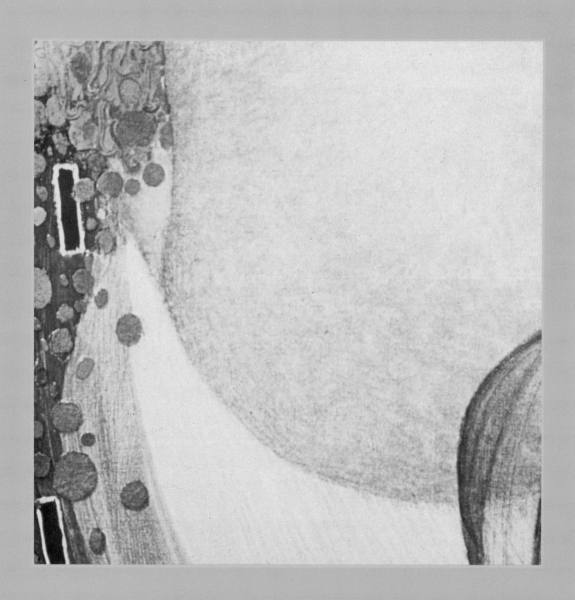

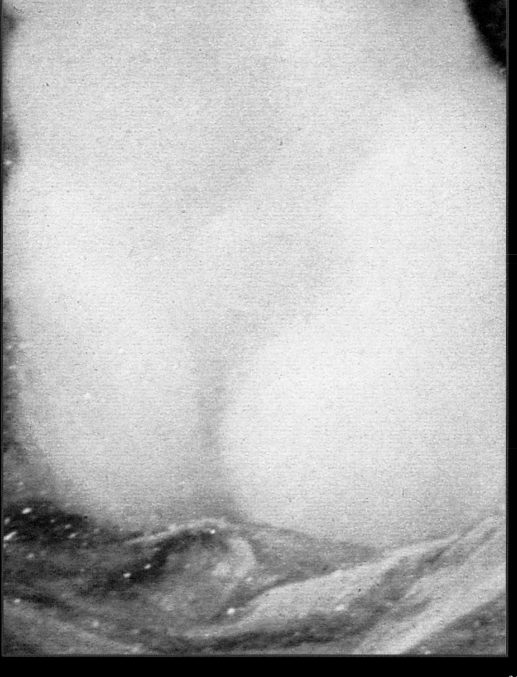

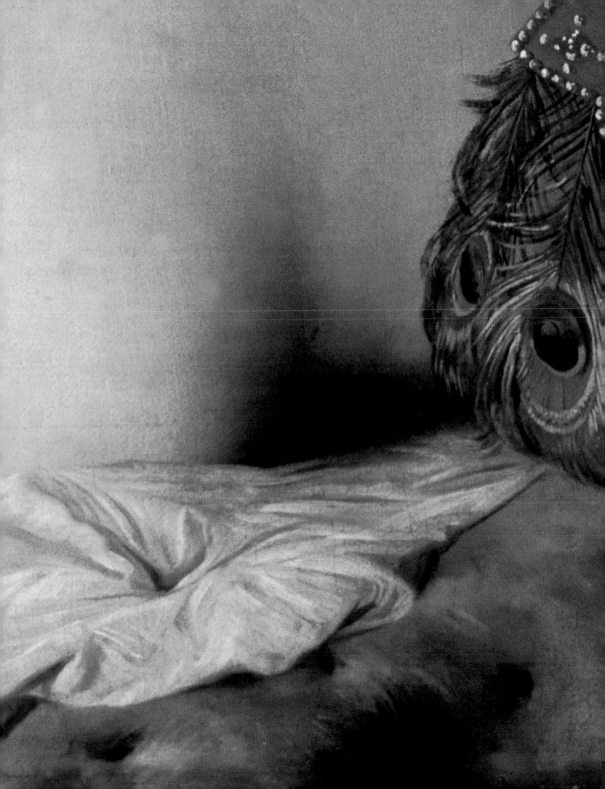

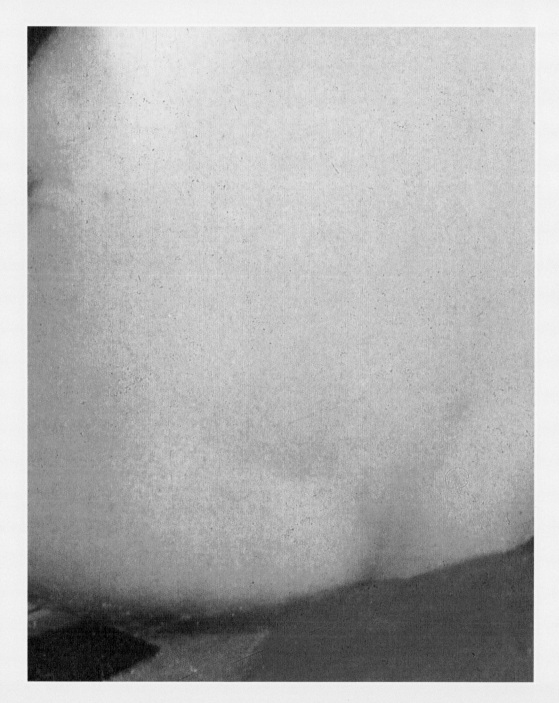

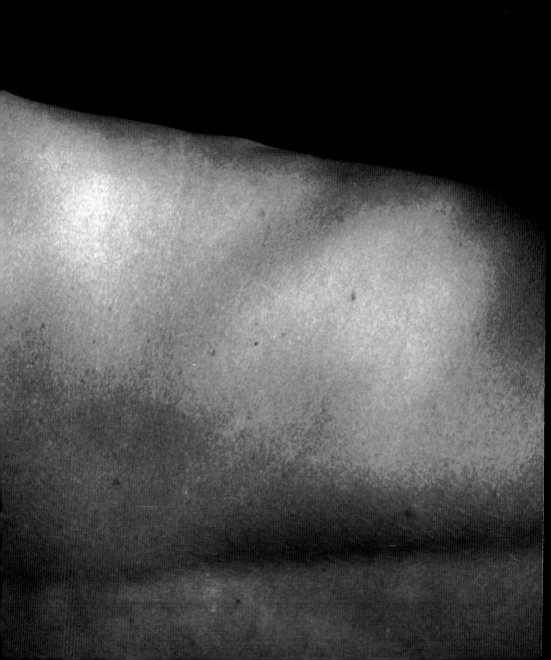

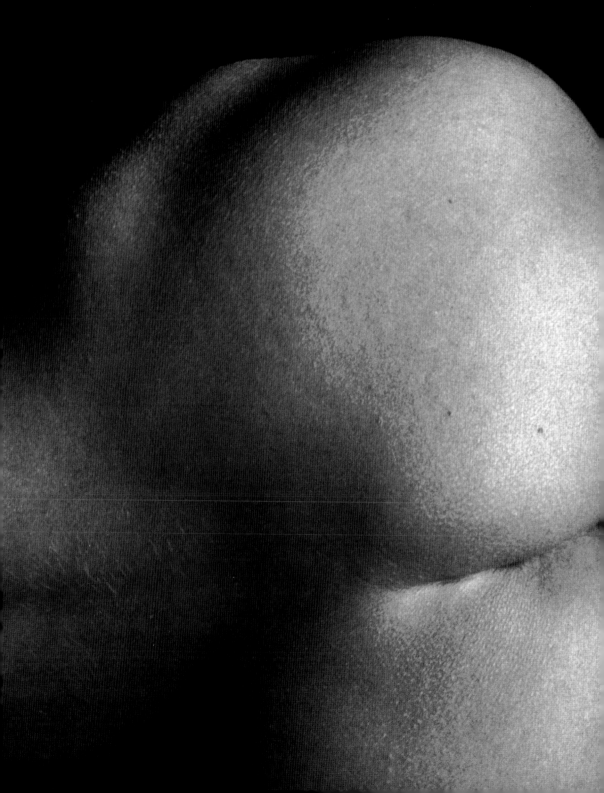

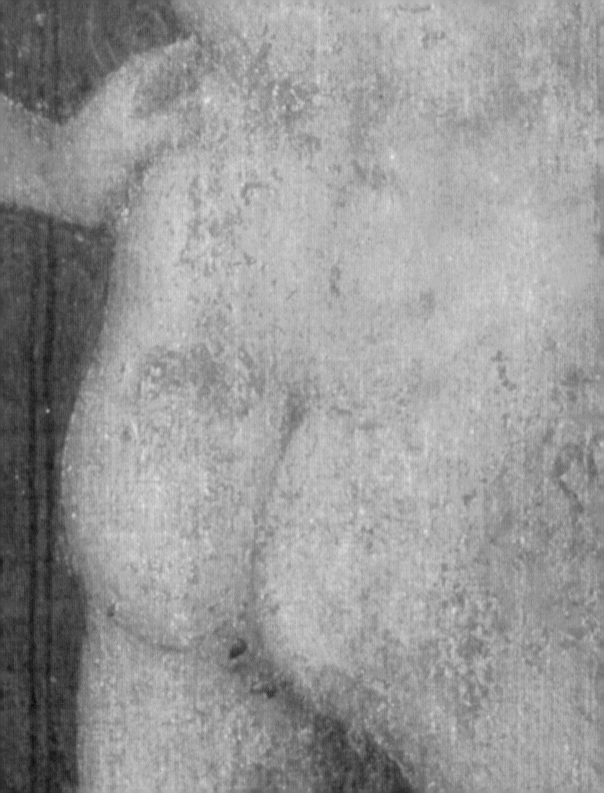

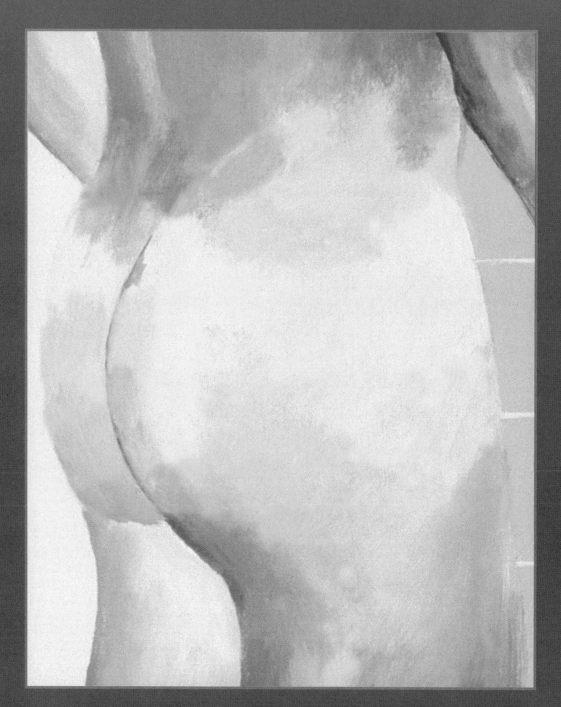

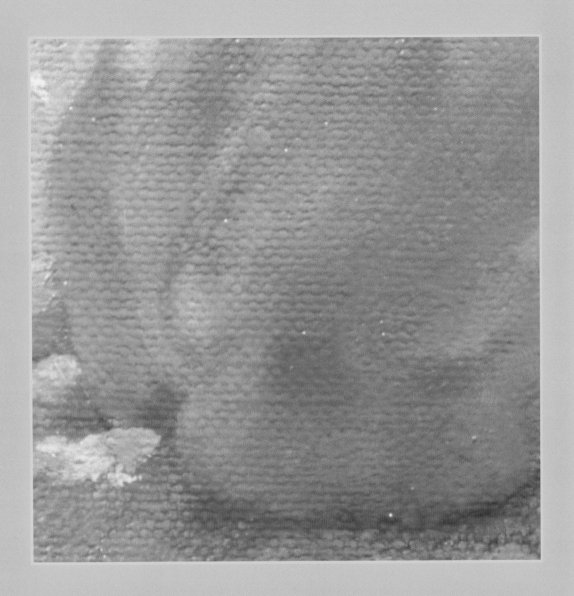

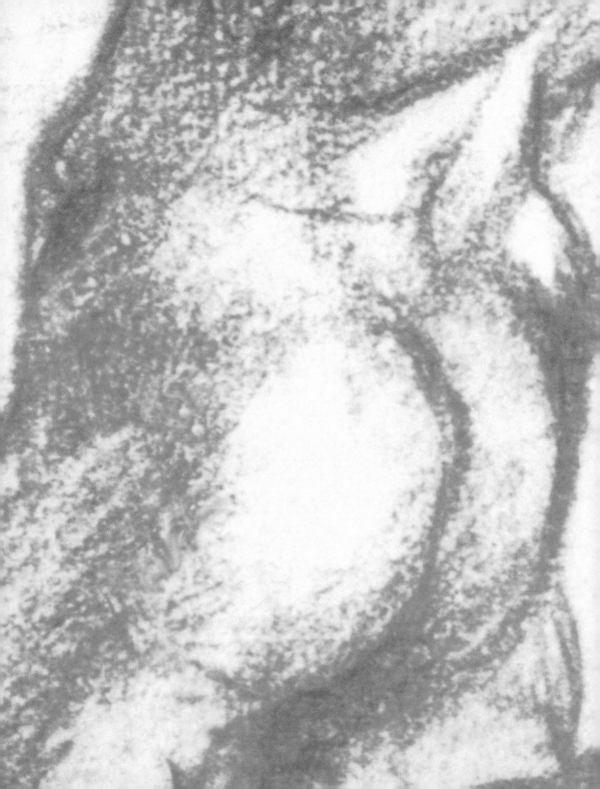

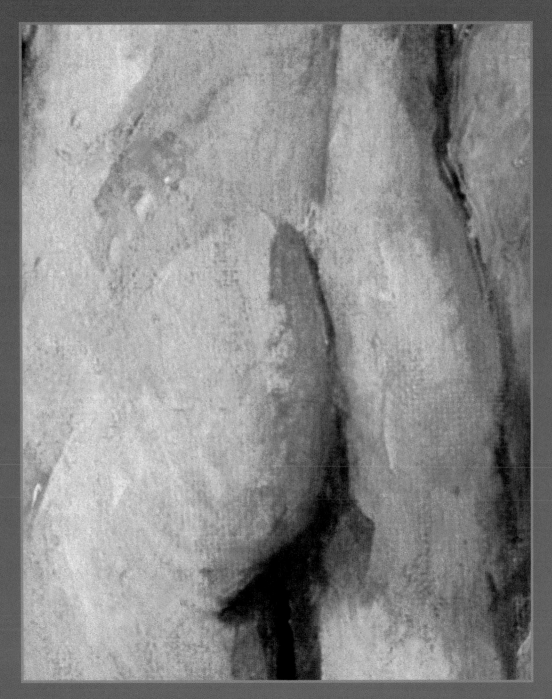

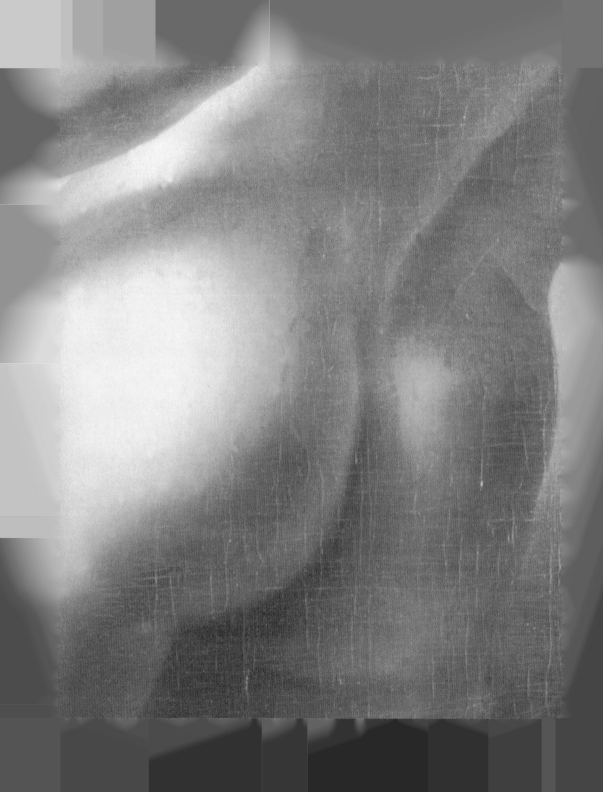

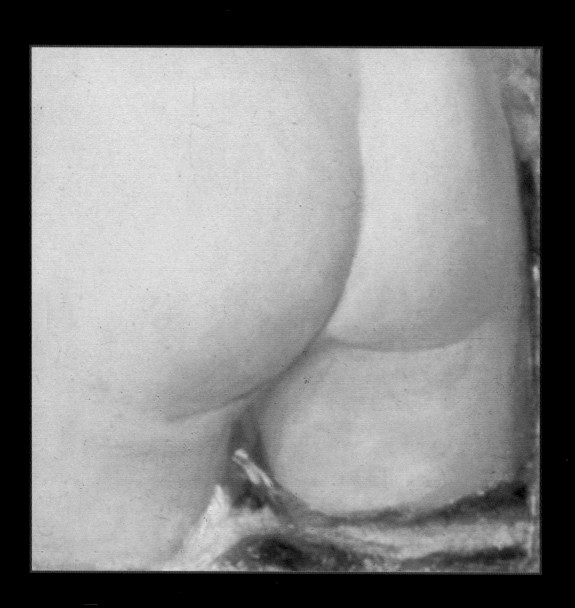

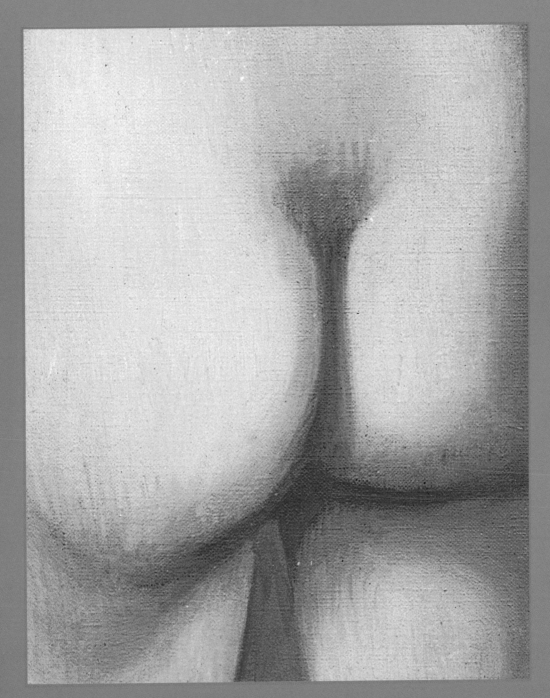

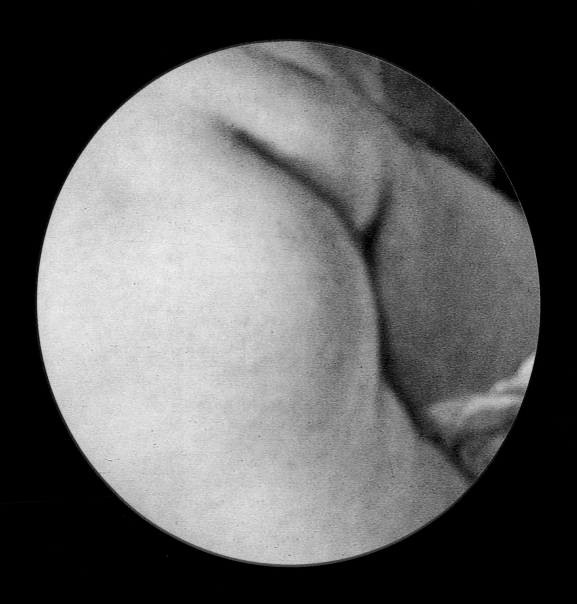

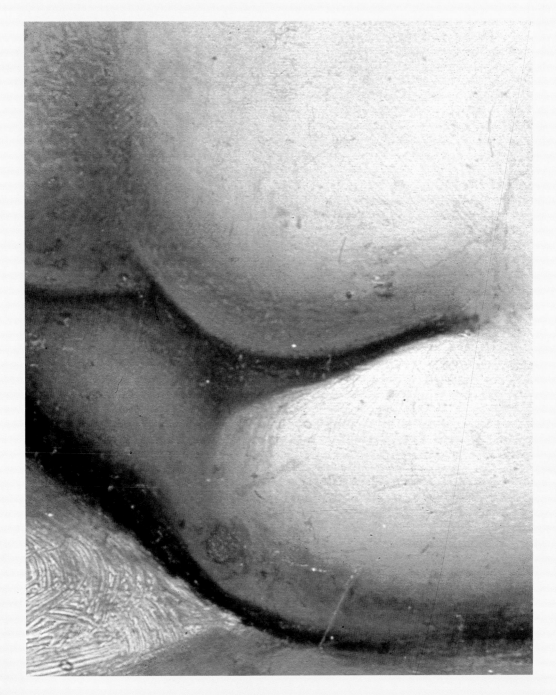

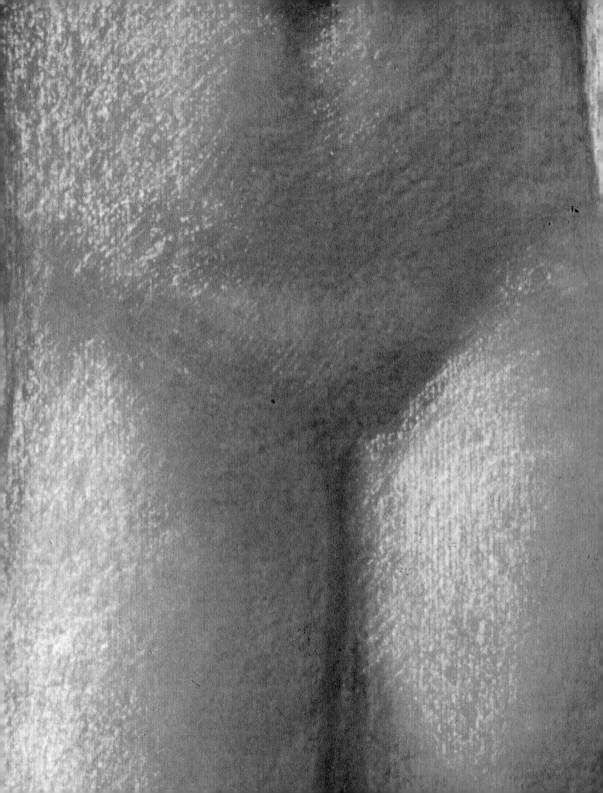

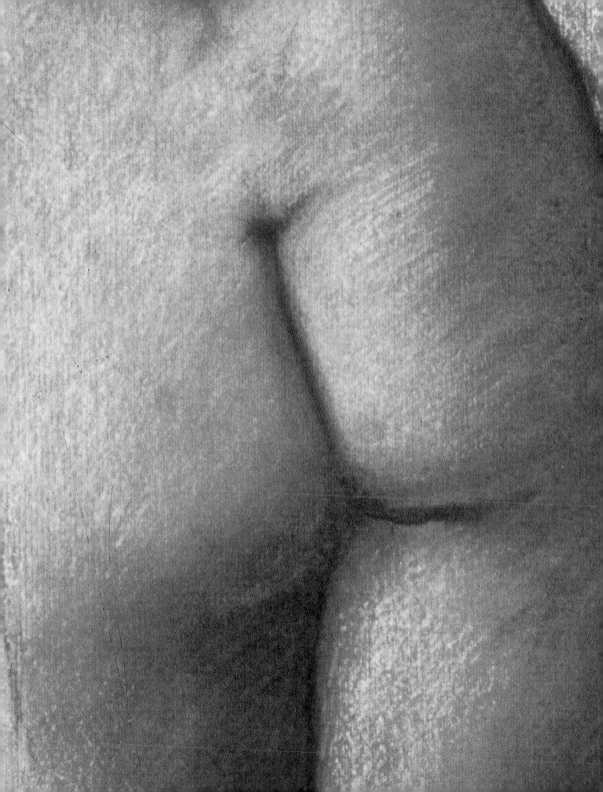

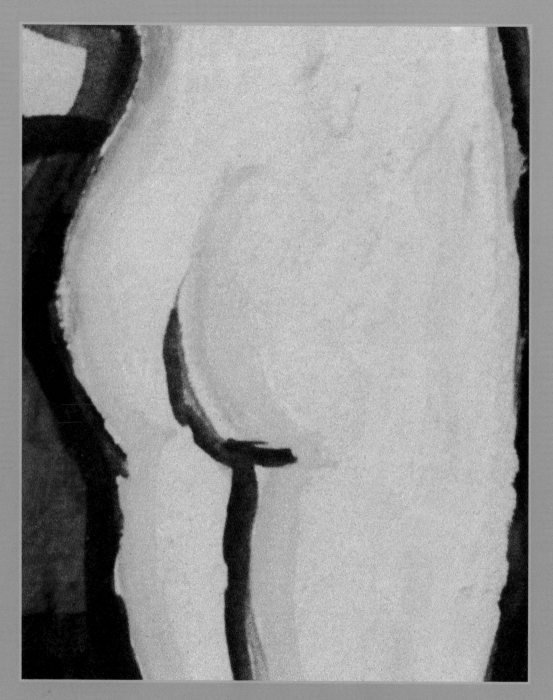

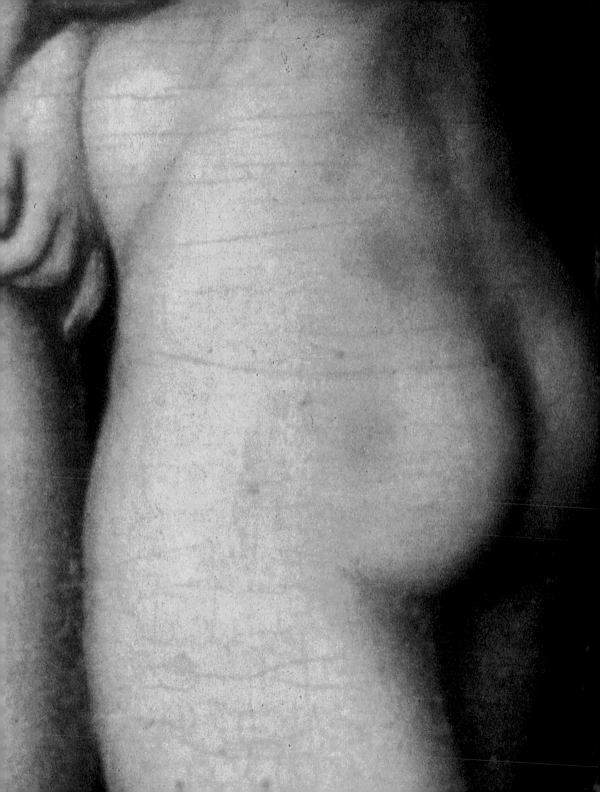

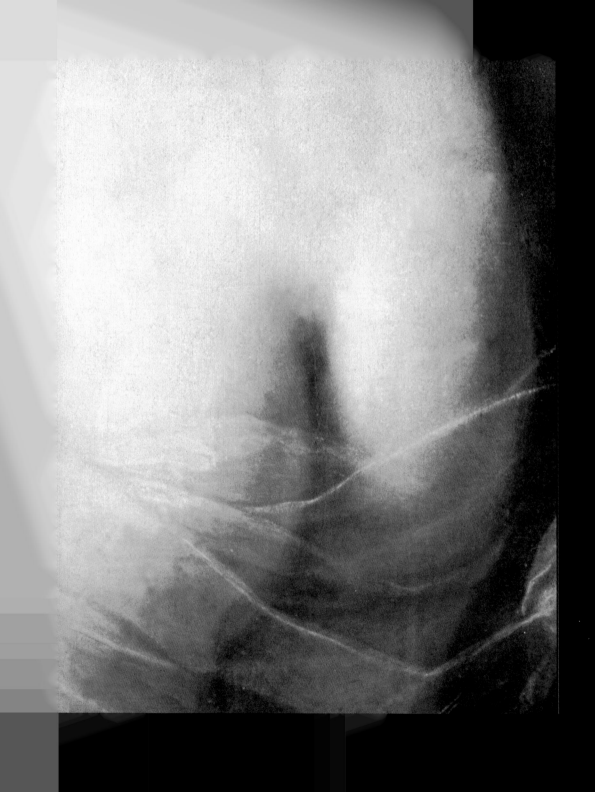

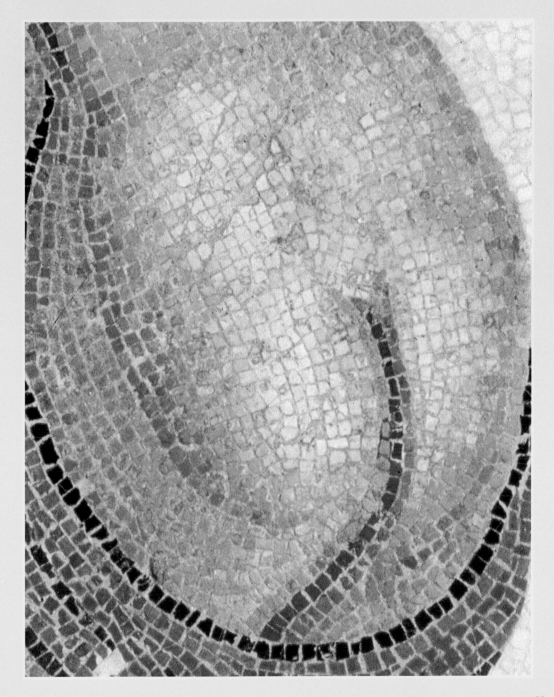

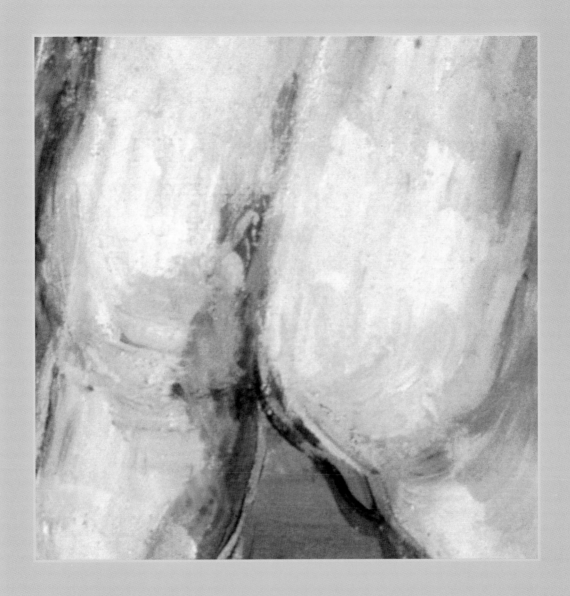

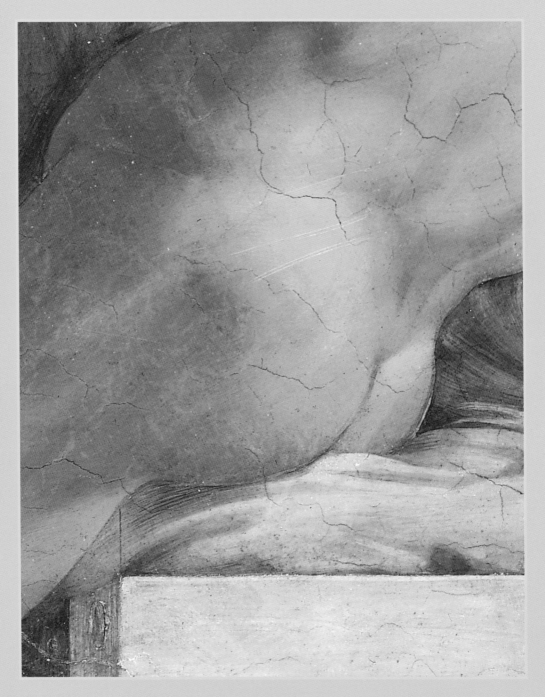

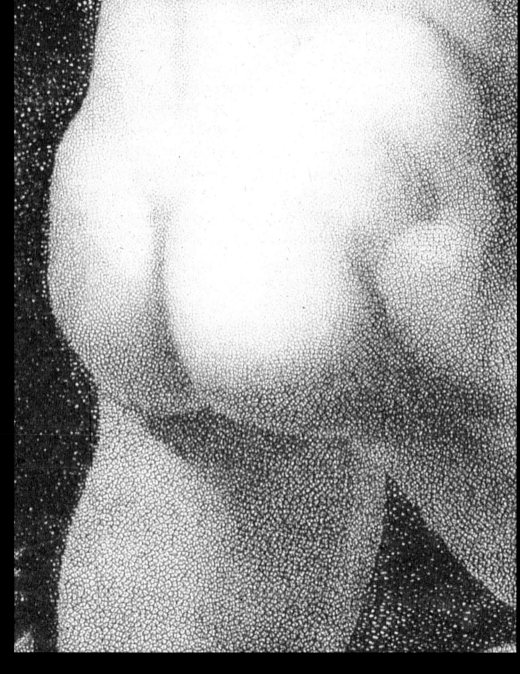

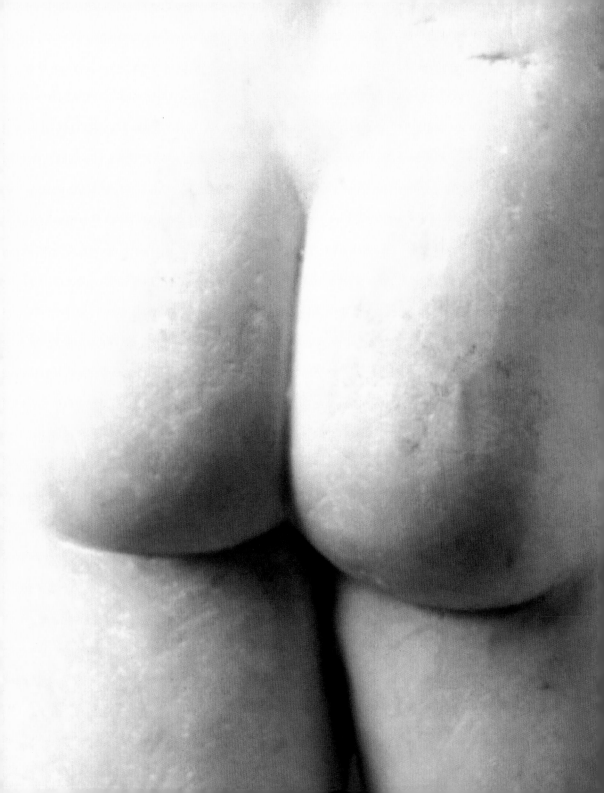

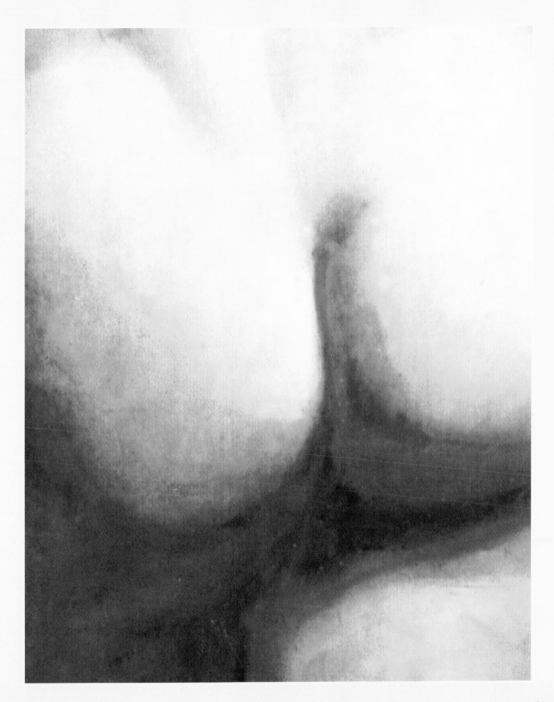

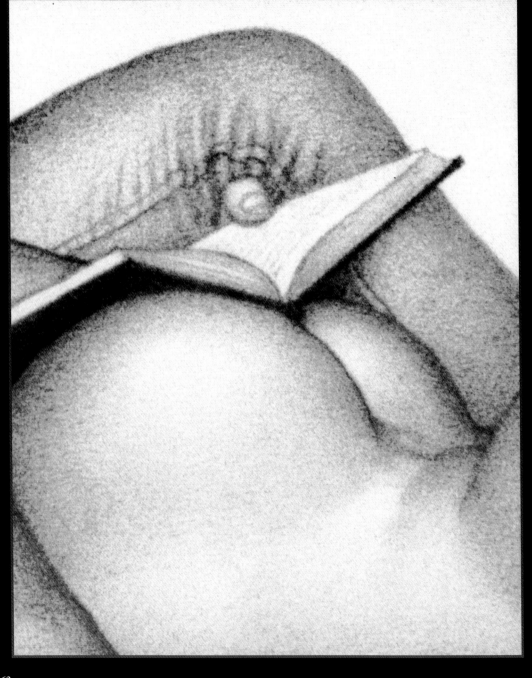

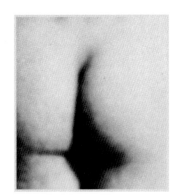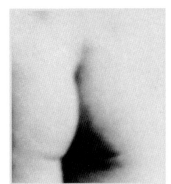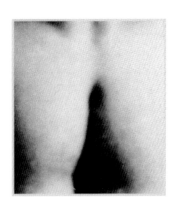

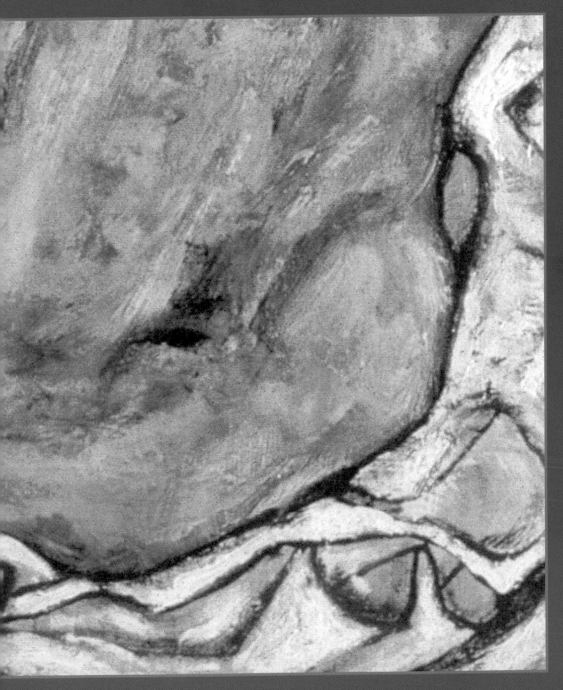

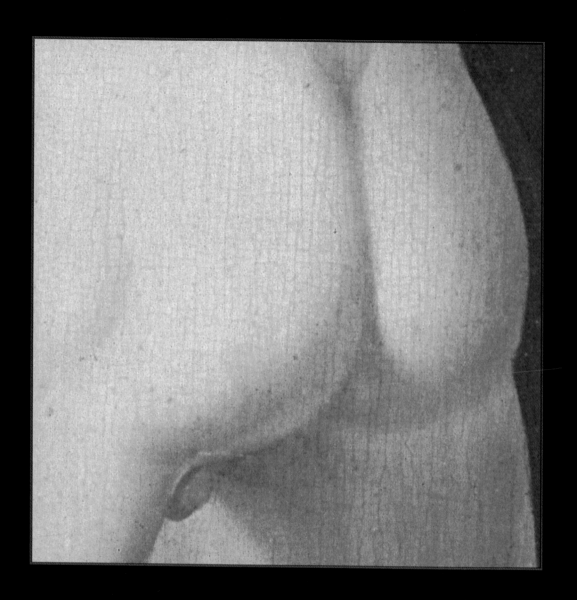

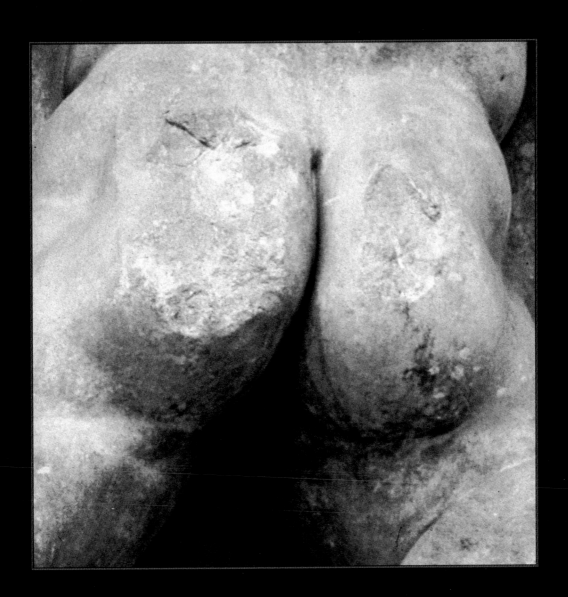

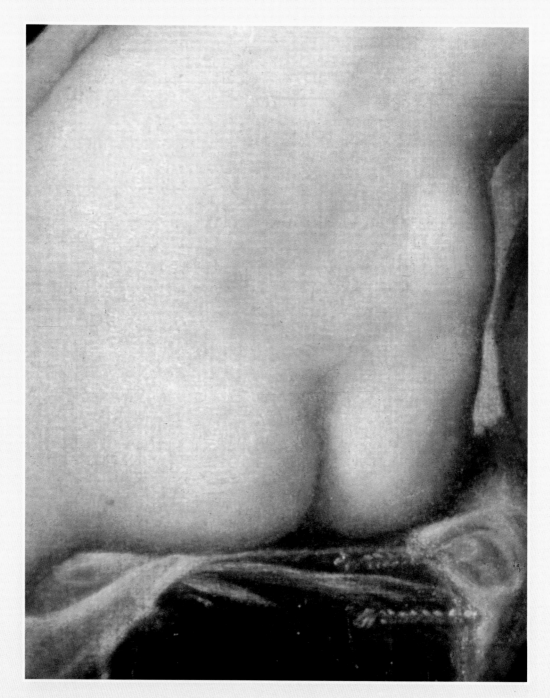

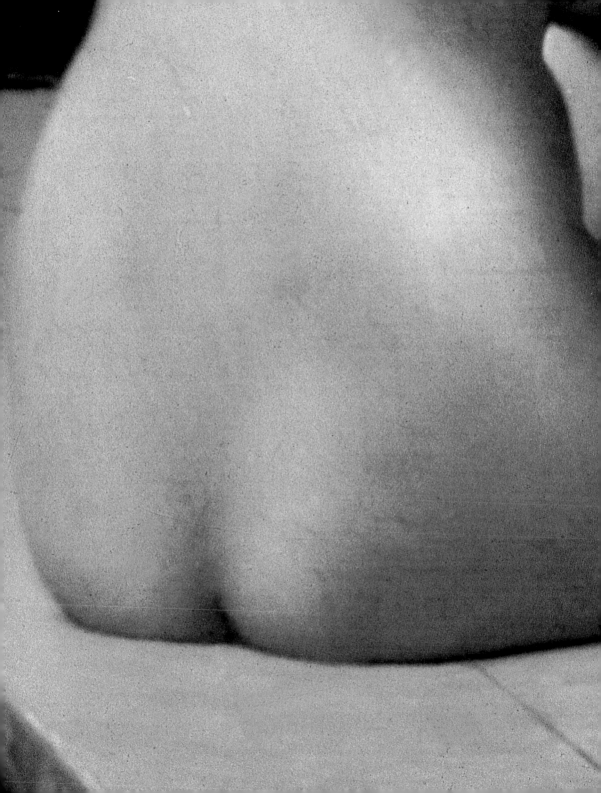

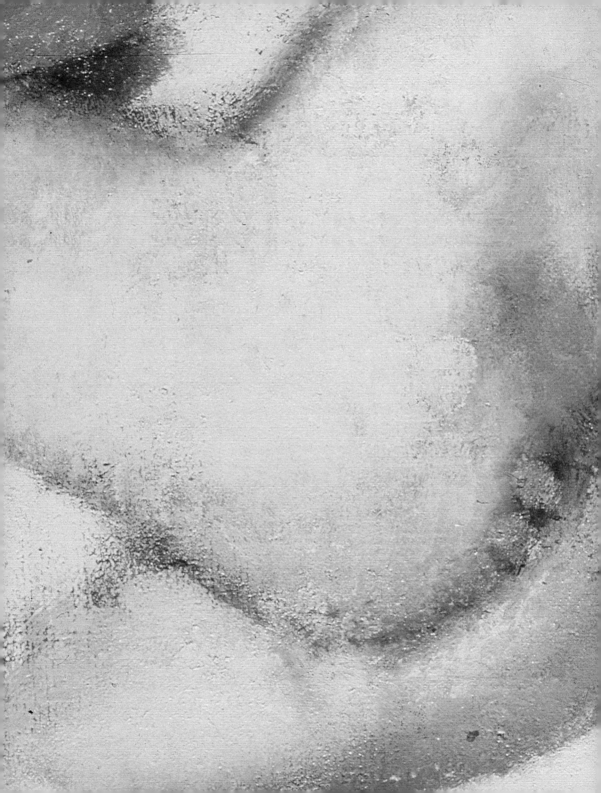

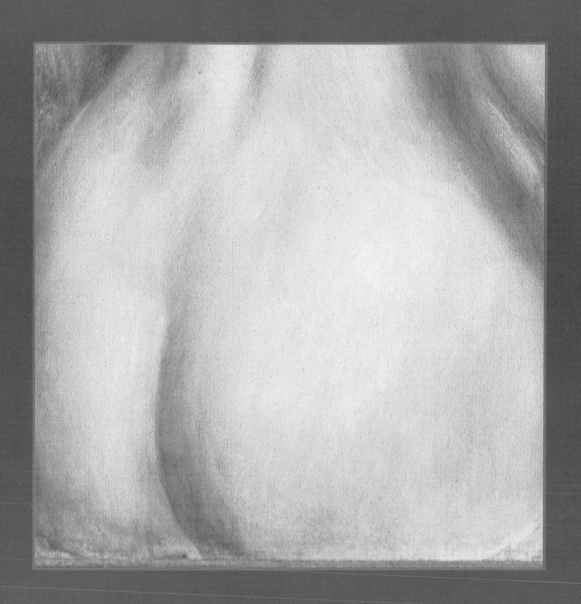

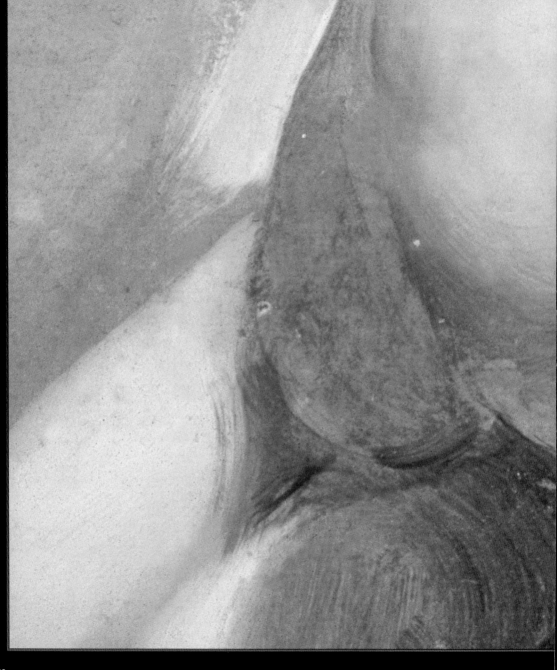

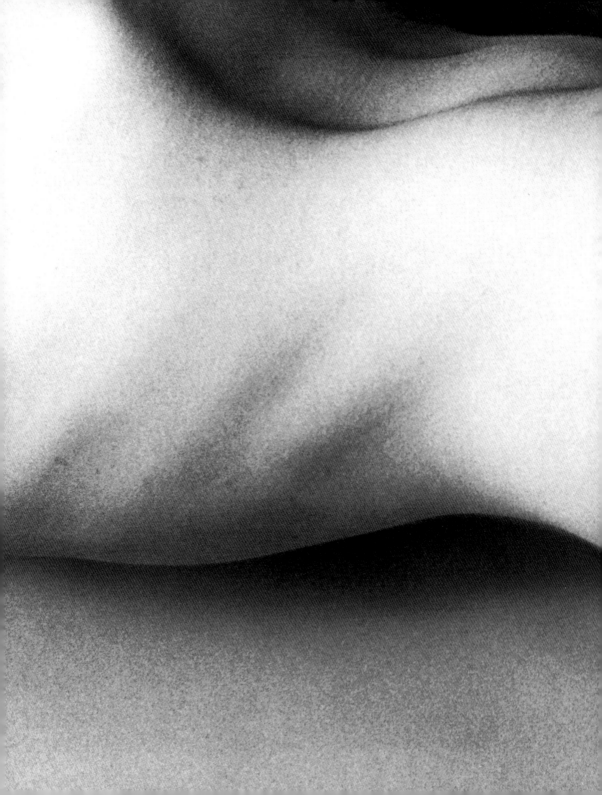

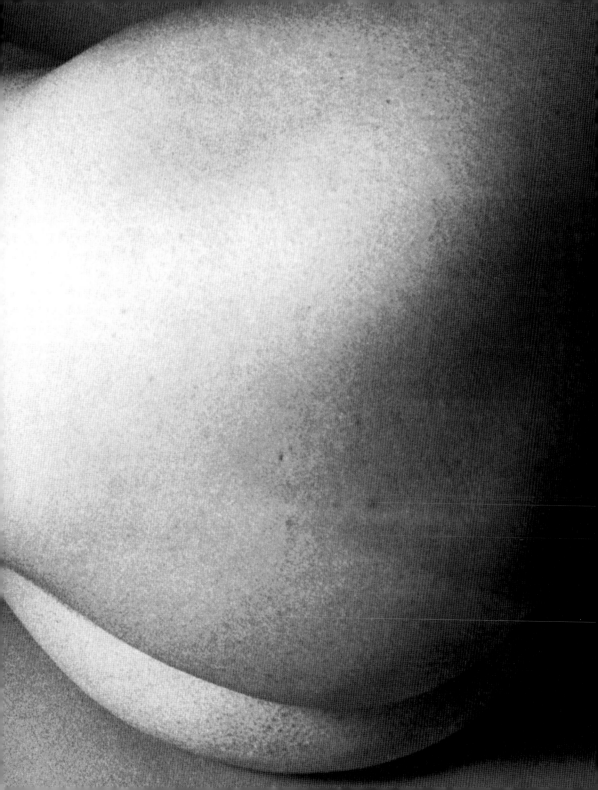

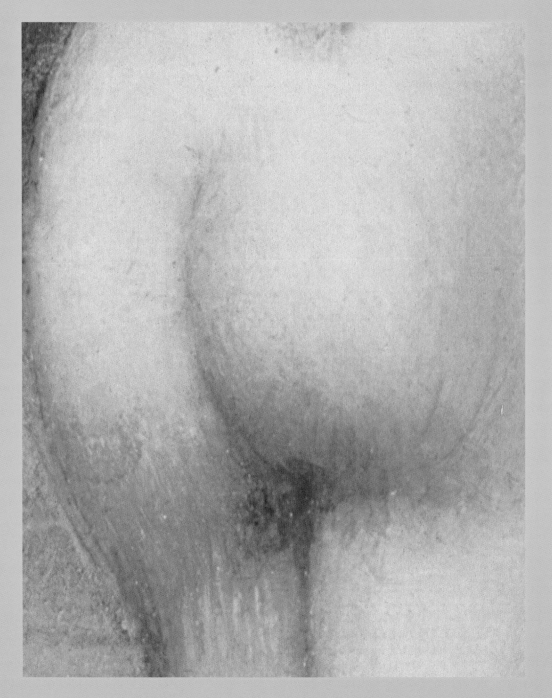

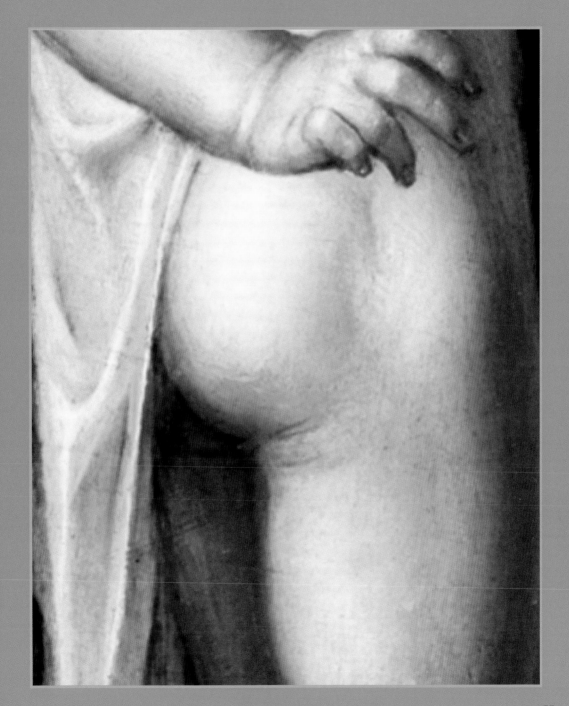

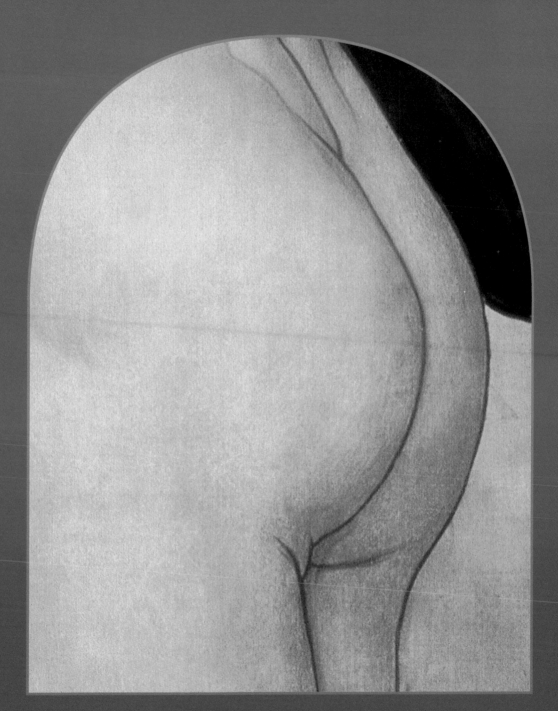

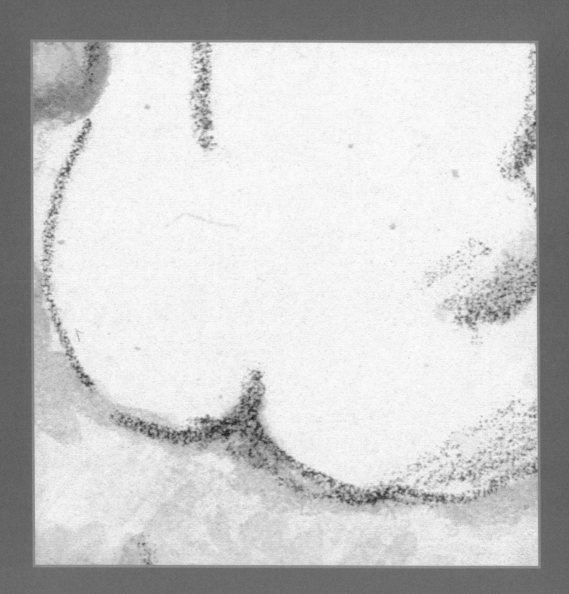

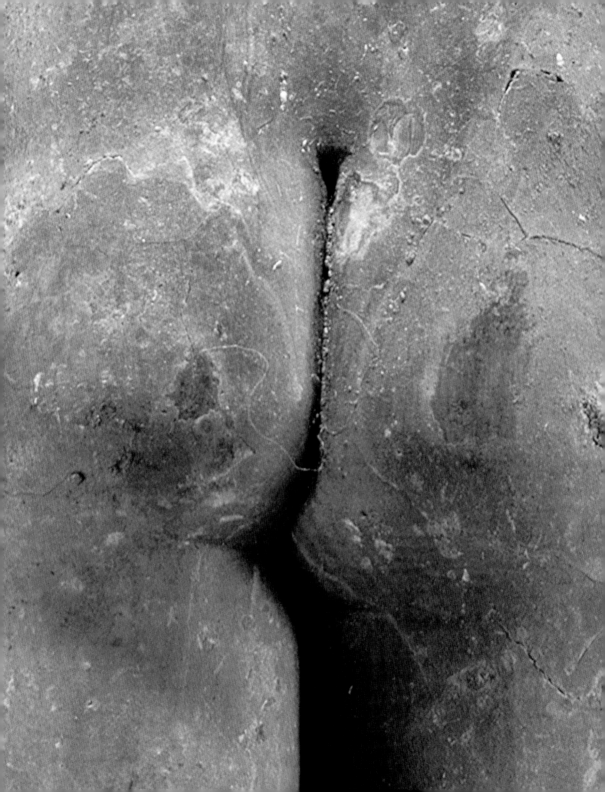

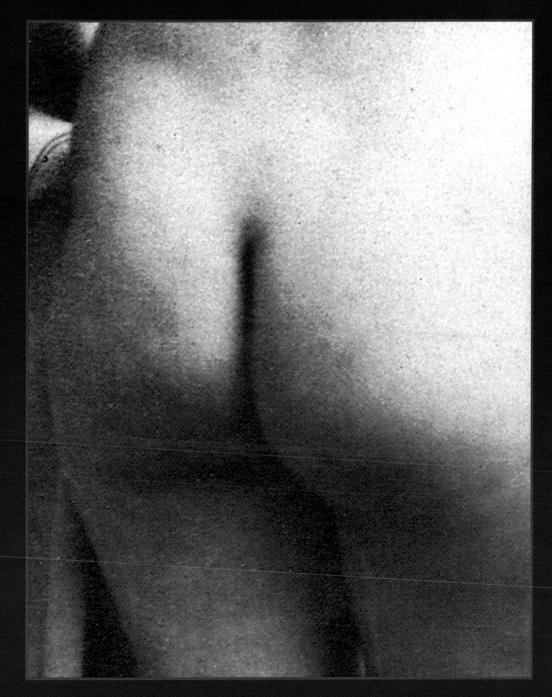

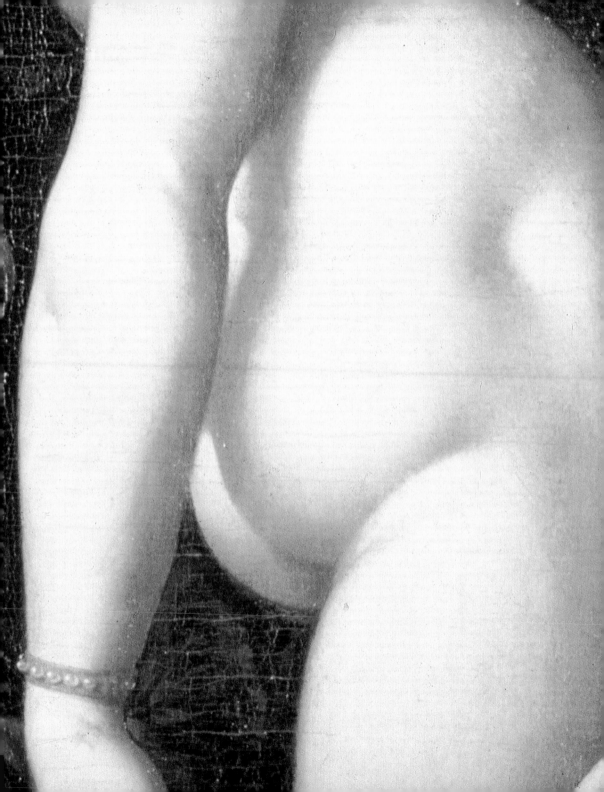

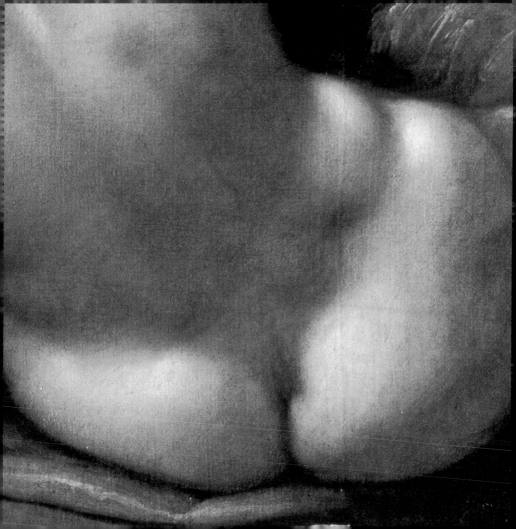

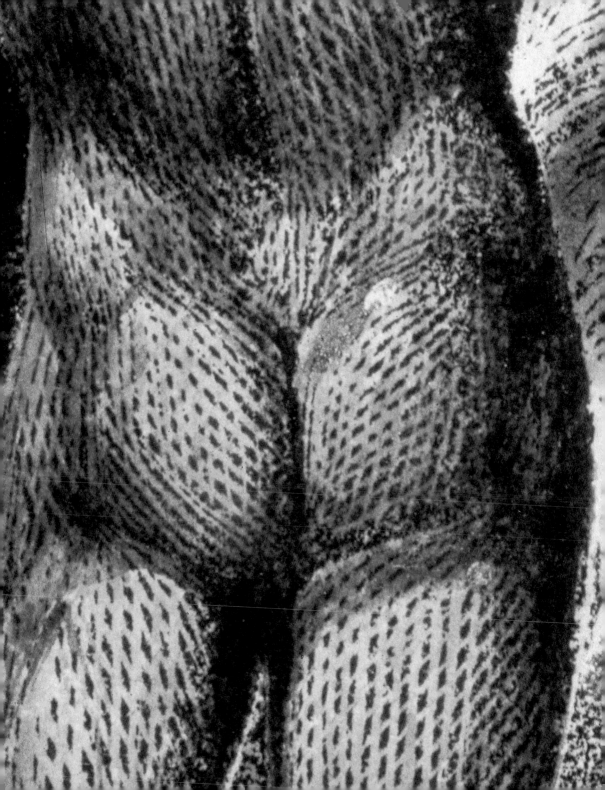

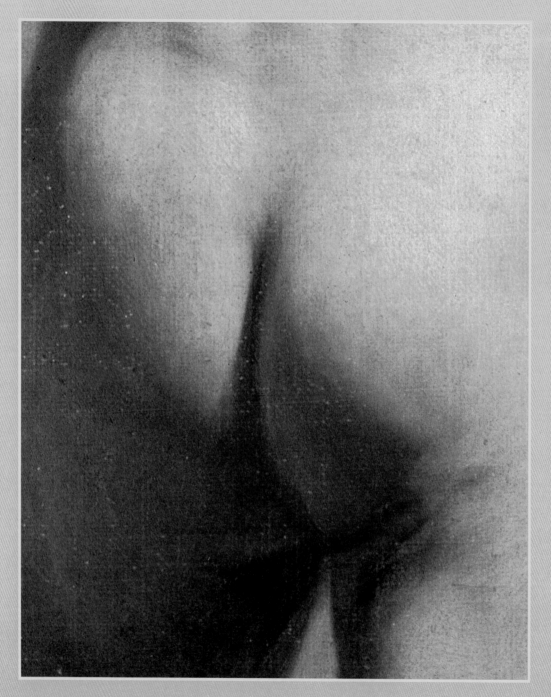

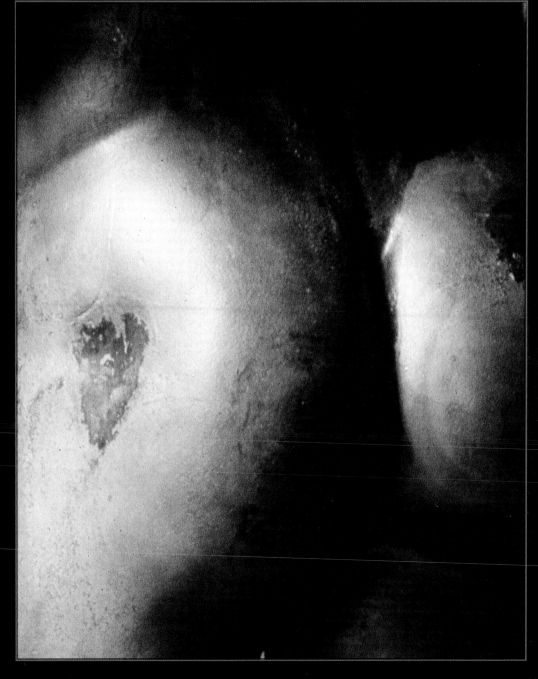

93

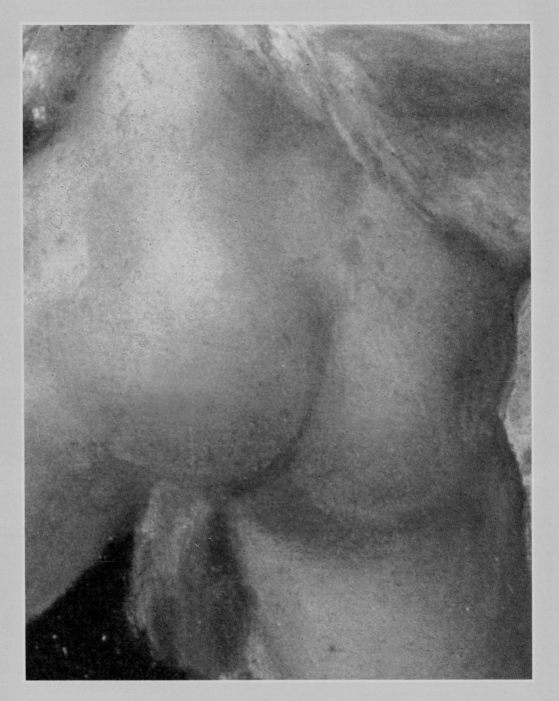

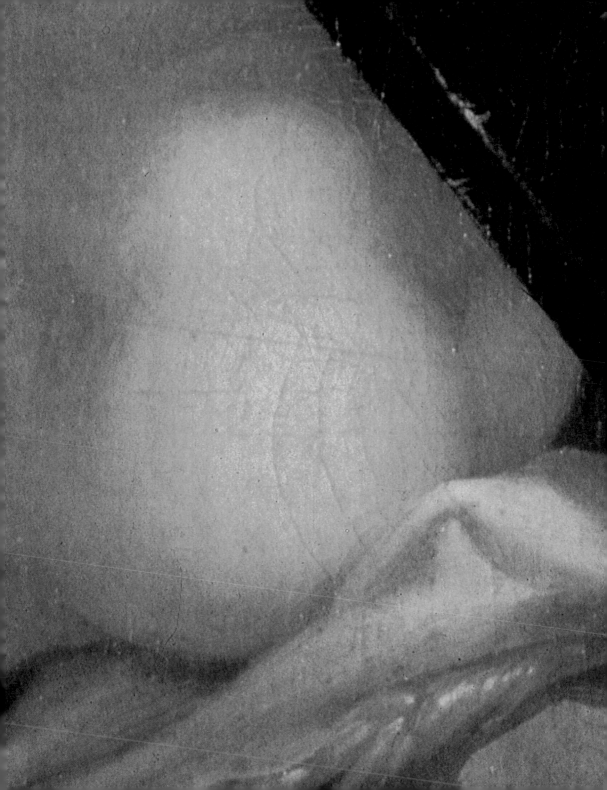

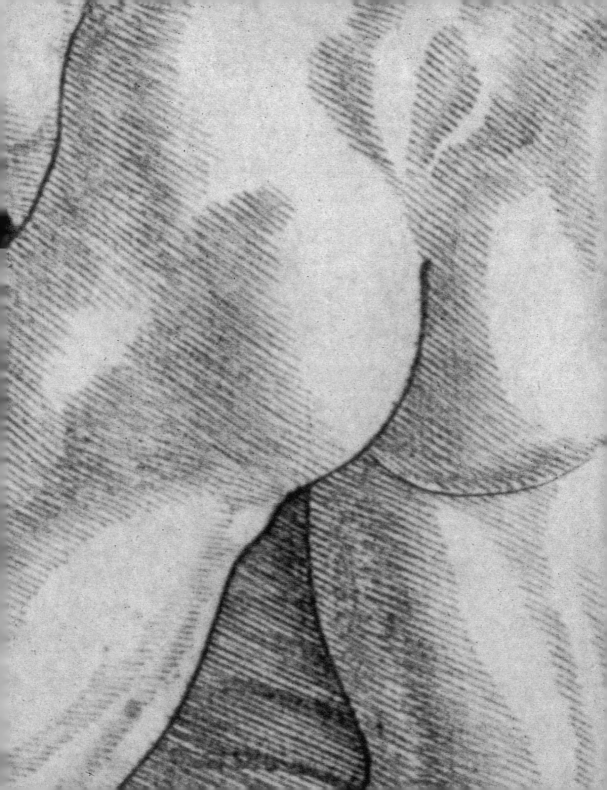

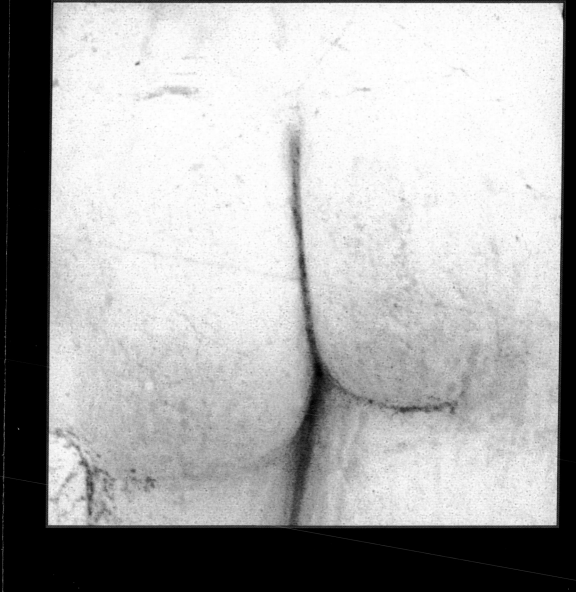

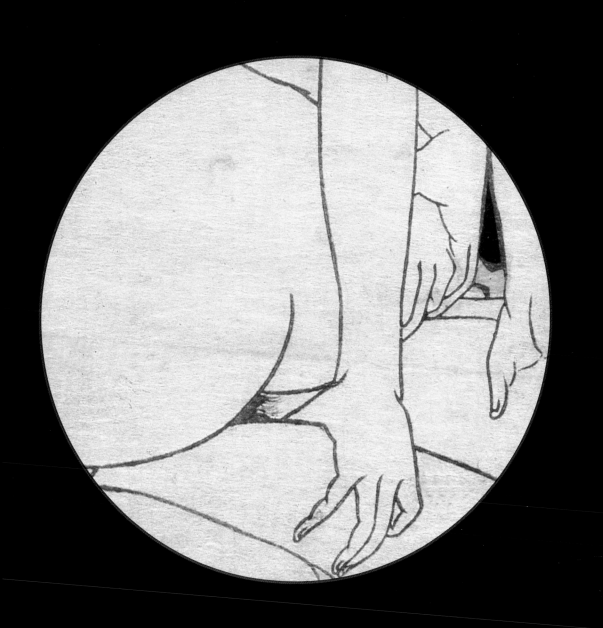

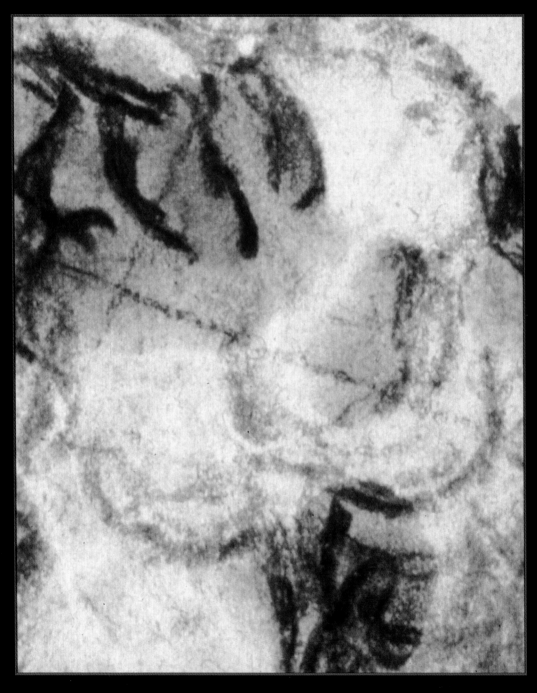

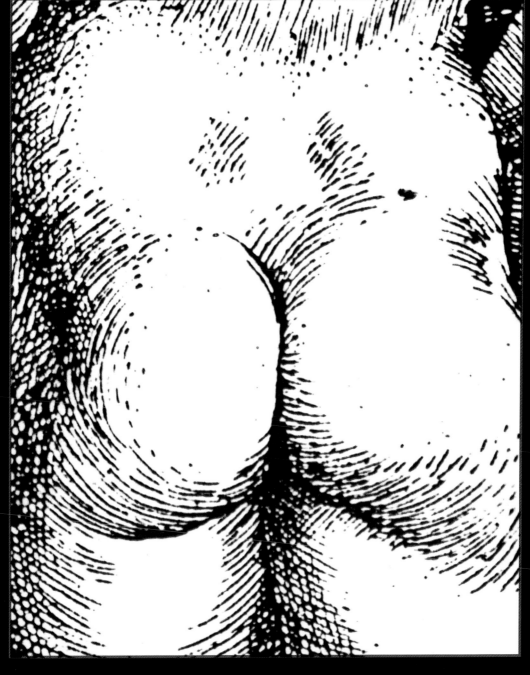

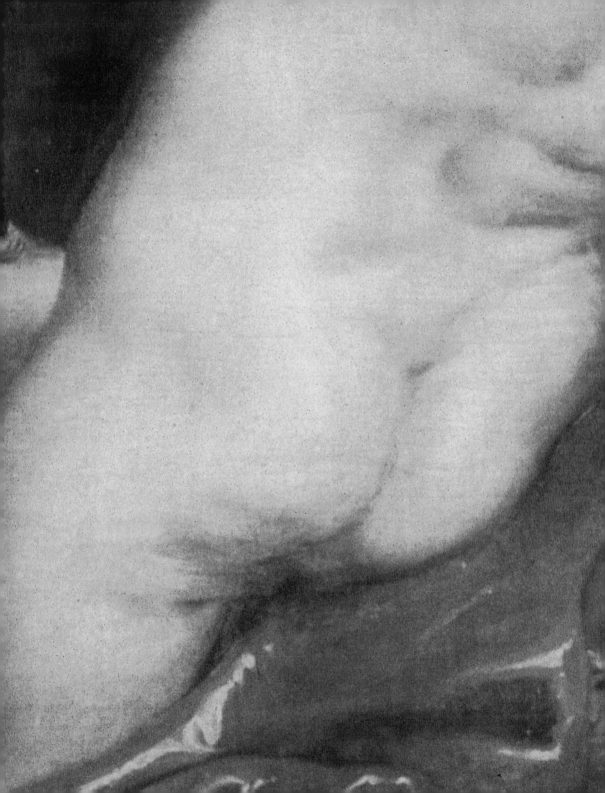

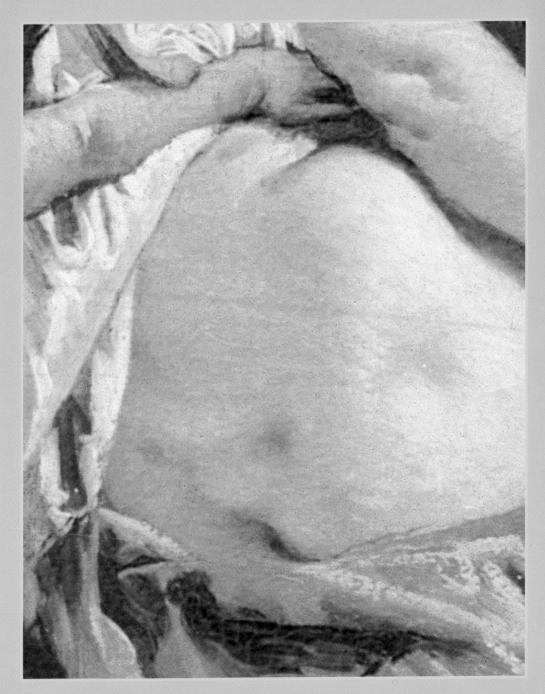

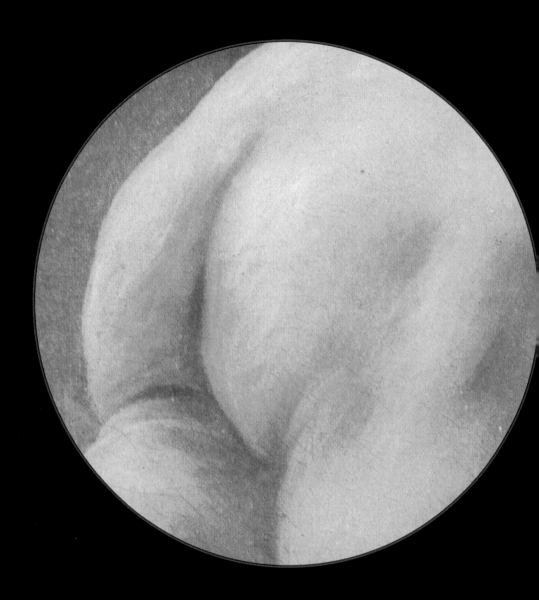

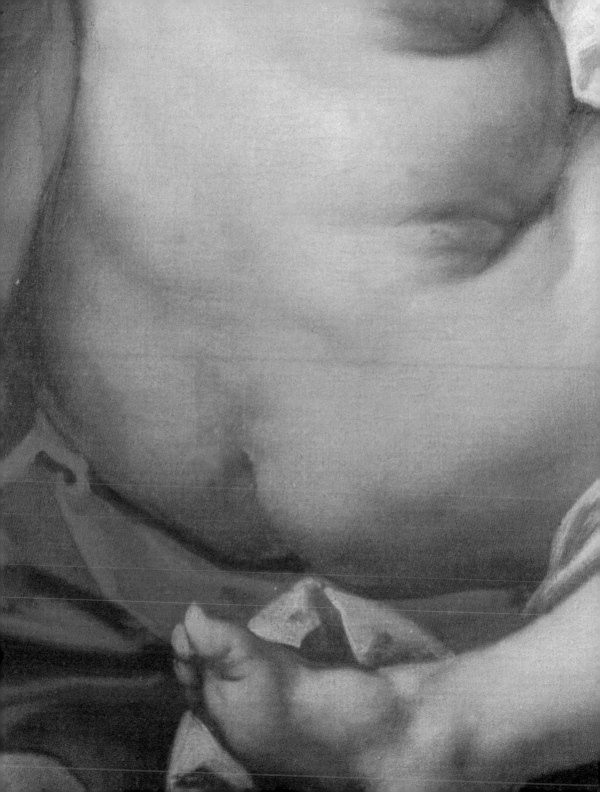

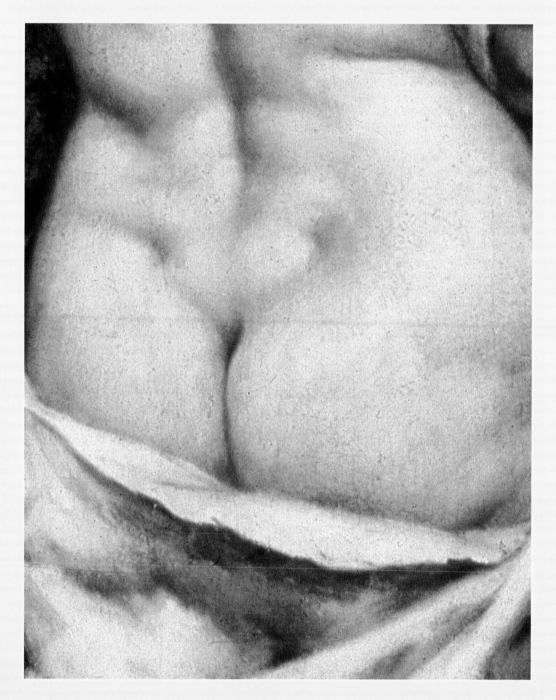

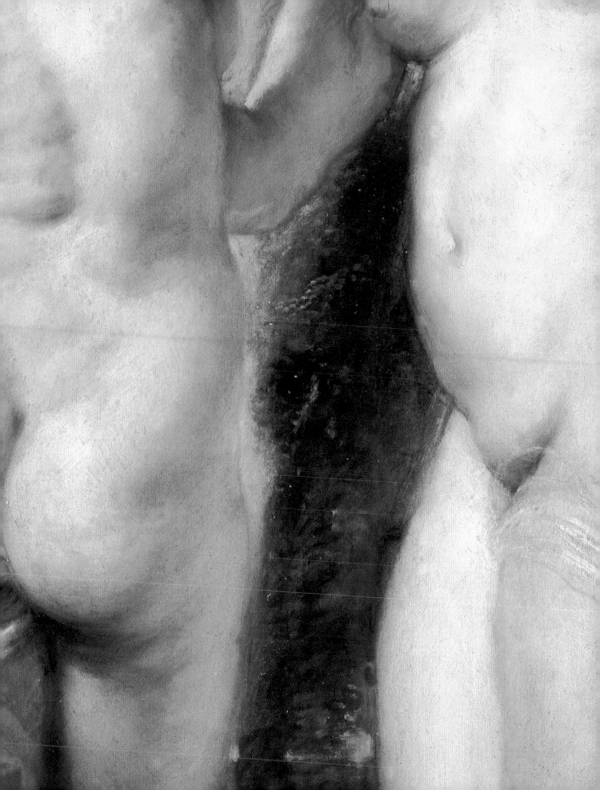

the full picture

(above and pages 10–11)

TWO BOYS IN A POOL
David Hockney (b. 1937)
Acrylic on canvas
1965

A hedonistic depiction of outdoor living, this painting from Hockney's Los Angeles incarnation celebrates with carefree innocence the nascent gay culture emerging on the West Coast. The boys' pale, untanned bottoms merge into the Op Art acrylic swirls of water reflection.

(above and pages 6, 12)

BATHYLLUS POSTURING
Aubrey Beardsley (1872–98)
Engraving
1896

This is an illustration taken from the Sixth Satire of Juvenal (c. A.D. 55–c. 140), the Roman stoic and satirist who wrote sixteen verse satires attacking Roman decadence, extravagance, and unnatural vices. The sixth reflected Juvenal's misogyny and his anti-Semitism. This illustration by Beardsley, done two years before his early death at the age of just twenty-six, shows Bathyllus, a figure of ambiguous gender, literally giving a finger to polite society.

(above and page 13)

FULL BACK
William Fogg (b. 1953)
Charcoal on paper
1993

California artist Fogg specializes in meticulously excecuted figures and faces, for the most part done in charcoal and pastel. His work is often included in exhibitions that focus on both the classical approach to the figure and the fragmentation of body parts. One of the aspects with which he is fascinated is the bodybuilder/ poseur frozen moment in time. In this study he subtracts the extremities from the torso; all lines lead to the magnificently sculptural buttocks.

(above and page 14)

CUPID CARVING A BOW
Parmigianino (Girolamo Francesco Mazzola, 1503–40)
Oil on canvas
1535

Cupid (desire) is the Roman version of Eros, the love-child of Aphrodite and Ares. In his early avatars he was a powerful figure, but during the Hellenistic period (fourth to second century B.C.), when attention was diverted from Olympus to the doings of mortals, he dwindled into a childlike figure who flitted around firing gold-tipped arrows to inspire love at first sight, and lead-tipped arrows to incite instant loathing. The saucy, yet innocent bottom belongs to a naughty boy rather than a full-blown love-god.

(below and page 15)

THE ABDUCTION OF GANYMEDE
Peter Paul Rubens (1577–1640)
Oil on canvas
17th century

Ganymede was the beautiful boy whom Zeus, king of the gods, found so irresistible that, pausing only to assume the shape of an eagle, he snatched him up and took him to Mount Olympus to become the cup-bearer of the gods. Later, besotted Zeus placed Ganymede in the sky as the constellation Aquarius. Rubens, the acknowledged master of flesh in paint, has here rendered some almost palpable buttocks, but there may be a feeling that they are just a little too dimpled and curvaceous to be those of a teenage boy.

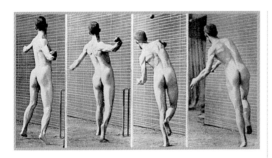

(above and pages 16–17)

**MAN BOWLING
IN CRICKET**
Eadweard Muybridge
(1830–1904)
Photographic print
1889

Howzat! Distinctly dangerous, if you are playing with a standard cricket ball—that's how. Muybridge's pioneering freeze-frame shots were designed to plot the way muscles move in action, hence the nudity.

(above and page 18)

THE THREE GRACES
Hans von Aachen (1552–1615)
Oil on canvas
c. 1604

In classical mythology the Three Graces (known as Charites in Latin) were agreeable but minor deities

embodying the virtues of beauty, gentleness, and friendship; they are usually considered handmaidens of Aphrodite and are so charmingly indistinct that no one knows quite how many there are, although three is the norm. In art, however, they are firm favorites, perhaps because they are always depicted au naturel.

(above and page 19)

**HERCULES
AND OMPHALE**
Bartholomeus Spranger
(1546–1611)
Oil on copper
c. 1575–80

Unlikely new man Hercules wields a distaff and gets in touch with his feminine side, while his mistress Omphale strikes a bold masculine pose in a fine piece of role-swapping. Omphale was queen of Lydia and bought Hercules as a

slave after he had completed his twelve labors. She made him wear women's clothes, yet he performed many mighty deeds on her behalf: killed the outlaw Syleus, destroyed a hideous serpent, and sacked the city of the enemy Itoni.

(above and page 20)

DANAË
Gustav Klimt (1862–1918)
Oil on canvas
1907–8

The beautiful Danaë writhes, apparently alone, in the gilded ecstasy that is typical of Klimt. According to Greek myth, Danaë was locked up in a tower of bronze by her father, who feared a prophecy that he would be killed by her son. Bronze towers meant nothing to Zeus, who came to her as a shower of gold; she then bore Perseus, slayer of Medusa.

(top right and page 21)

**DIANA AND HER NYMPHS,
WATCHED BY SATYRS**
Jan Brueghel the Elder
(1568–1625) and Hendrick
Balen the Elder (c. 1575–1632)
Oil on copper
c. 1620

Diana, goddess of the hunt, and her sturdy nymphs rest after a long day in the field. The results of their labors can be seen strewn out in front of them. Now the huntswomen

themselves are being stalked, as lascivious satyrs creep up on them and poke and snigger. Jan, one of the minor Brueghels, specialized in landscapes but also collaborated with the great Rubens, whose influence can be seen in the generous flesh of the goddess and her entourage.

(above and pages 22–23)

THE GRAND ODALISQUE
Jean-Auguste-Dominique
Ingres (1780–1867)
Oil on canvas
1814

Ingres was the Puritan to Delacroix's Cavalier in the nineteenth-century battle of Classicism vs. Romanticism. His flawlessly exact work depended on draftsmanship and precise vision. In his hands the Romantic craze for Orientalism, always an excuse for scarcely clad bodies, produced this immaculate, long-backed odalisque; although beautiful, it is difficult to imagine her rumpling the sheets or abandoning herself to physical pleasures.

(above and page 24)

**WOMAN AFTER
THE BATH**

Goyo Hasiguchi (1880–1921)
Color woodblock print
1920

A late print from a prolific Japanese artist—simple in design and evidently strongly influenced by the Western canon, which was becoming increasingly well known in Japan at the time. Anatomically precise, the focus of a straight-forward composition, this Japanese lady seems caught between Eastern and Western cultures. Total nudity is unusual in Japanese painting.

(above and page 25)

THE TURKISH BATH

Jean-Auguste-Dominique Ingres
(1780–1867)
Oil on canvas
1862

Acres of flesh but no steam in Ingres' version of a Turkish bath, a telling example of how, in some hands, more can be less. Ingres was much influenced by the early shots at photography, approving of the rigid pose the sitter had to adopt. The careful composition of many bodies reflects this interest, although there are overtones of a modern vacation snap of "beach-babes." At the front is Ingres' favorite long-backed model. There is the careful impression of languor, but none of the sweatiness of the bath-house.

(above and page 26)

MORS IN LUTETIA 2

E. F. Kitchen (b. 1951)
Photographic print
1997

An American photographer in Paris, Kitchen took this shot as one of a series of self-portraits in an auto-biographical photo-essay. She began her career in the cinema, and the carefully composed shot and props have the air of a scene from a narra-tive film. Shot with available light in a Paris apartment, the prints were developed using the platinum/palladium process, which makes each image a unique art piece. The title of this study means "Death in Paris," which can be construed as metaphor rather than actuality.

(above and page 27)

**NUDE PORTRAIT
OF MISS VERNON**

E.O. Hoppé (1878–1972)
Photographic print
1924

The delicious and anonymous Miss Vernon is presented almost as an abstract shape against a dark background. The composition masks out head and lower limbs, making her appear at first glance to be a statue from antiquity. However, the curve of her back and slouch of the shoulder are more inviting to the touch than cold marble.

(below and pages 28–29)

NUDE

Brett Weston (1911–94)
Gelatin silver print
1979

The second son of Edward Weston, Brett followed in his father's photo-graphic footsteps, exhibiting major works from the age of seventeen.

This monumental nude comes from late in his career. Its subliminal sexual ambiguity—the roundness of the buttocks, the smooth shaft of the back, and the long, prominent ridge of the spine—tugs intriguingly at the mind. Is it a female nude or a stylized vision of male genitalia? Is it both?

(above and page 30)

**FOUR MALE
NUDE FIGURES**

Pietro Perugino (Pietro
Vannucci, c. 1450–1523)
Oil on canvas
c. 1505

One look at this picture and you would think yourself on the West Coast. The poses of the men are familiar from paintings and photographs from the gay scene. However, this was painted in the sixteenth century by an Italian: the drooping posture and tilt of the head are characteristic of the artist Perugino.

(above and page 31)

BOY ABOUT TO TAKE A SHOWER

David Hockney (b. 1937)

Acrylic on canvas

1964–9

Another of Hockney's sun-kissed nudes from his California/Swimming Pool era. The dazzling whiteness of the boy's buttocks (protected by his bathingsuit while tanning) against the bronze of his skin draws the eye irresistibly. The subject's head is cropped off, reinforcing the hedonism of this painting—he is truly a sex object, with no individuality to hinder instant gratification: a thing of beauty, but not necessarily a joy forever.

(above and page 32)

THE CRITICS

Henry Scott Tuke (1858–1929)

Oil on canvas

1927

In contrast to Hockney's anonymous, decorative pool-boys, these whole-some chaps obviously have a life outside the painting, and an unambiguous narrative within it. Their burgeoning sexuality is not apparent to them, and they are not posing in a consciously provocative manner. Once you step back from the "bare" aspect, what dominates the work is the light and the sparkle of water in the little bay. Compare it with the stylized, abstract water patterns of a Hockney pool and you can see the diametrically opposed approaches that two artists have taken toward what is essentially the same subject.

(above and page 33)

NAKED SEATED MAN

Pierre Subleyras (1699–1749) (attrib.)

Oil on canvas

18th century

Seen in its entirety, this picture of a well-muscled nude male slightly loses its aura of eroticism and becomes more of an exercise in form and volume. Maybe it is because the composition diminishes the powerful body by squashing it into a small "box." The focus becomes the broad, muscled back. The flesh tones are well rendered, but the figure is no longer exciting, perhaps because it is uncertain what he is doing: he could be cutting his toenails.

(below and page 34)

STUDY OF A MAN NUDE

Andrea del Sarto (d'Agnolo, 1486–1530)

Chalk on paper

16th century

Andrea del Sarto was one of the most influential painters in sixteenth-century Florence. His draftsmanship was much influenced by Michelangelo (1475–1564), as can be seen in this chalk drawing of a muscular man. This is an unusual work for him; he is best known for his frescoes and for his role in Robert Browning's biographical poem.

(above right and page 35)

THE BATHERS

Paul Cézanne (1839–1906)

Oil on canvas

c. 1890–2

Late in his long career Cézanne returned to some of his earlier obsessions, one of which was the subject of bathers. His enduring fascination was really with setting figures in a landscape; bathing simply gave them an excuse to be there. He painted several bathing pictures, using both male and female models. This is an all-male version, well choreographed and featuring modern gents' underwear.

(below and page 36)

BOREAS ABDUCTING OREITHYIA

Joseph Ferdinand Lancrenon (1794–1874)

Oil on canvas

1822

This splendid pair of butt-cheeks belongs to Boreas, god of the north wind. He courted Oreithyia, daughter of King Erechtheus and Queen Praxithea of Athens. Oreithyia would have none of him, but one day he found her dancing besides the Ilyssus River in Athens, snatched her up in a cloud, and bore her to Thrace. She produced two winged sons (later Argonauts) and two daughters.

(above and page 37)

**PUTTI PLAYING WITH
GARLANDS OF FRUIT**
after Peter Paul Rubens
(1577–1640)
Oil on canvas
Undated

Putti are Cupid's little hench-persons, often seen in the background of his more impor-tant allegorical adventures. Here they have the canvas all to themselves and are shown tumbling around out of school. They are always slightly disturbing because they have the roly-poly bodies of infants but the knowing leers of old men.

(below and pages 38–39)

DAHLIA #1
Steven Lungley (b. 1953)
Photographic print
1999

Lungley is a Canadian artist who began his career in graphic design and film-making. This image is the

first in a series of nudes photographed in available light, using a 60-watt bulb and the simplest of atmos-pheres, in contrast to a previous essay, Meticulous Series, which used highly controlled light, props, and design. The image exploits natural contours, light, and shadow, which feel more sponta-neous and erotic. The relaxed slump of the model's unfocused shoulders suggests delicious postcoital fatigue.

(above and page 40)

THE BATHERS
Pierre-Auguste Renoir
(1841–1919)
Oil on canvas
1887

Another Impressionist has a stab at the subject of bathers (particularly female ones). This time it is Renoir, who, as usual, produces a charming picture, but it has the unmistakable feeling of the studio about it. In contravention of Impressionist prin-ciples, it was not entirely painted outside, directly from life—only Paul Cézanne (1839–1906) caught his death braving the elements with his easel. Although pretty, the girls have little life to them, and there is no trace of the elemental power found in Cézanne's work on the same subject.

(above and page 41)

NUDE
Henry Montassier (b. 1880)
Oil on canvas
20th century

Except for the subject's nudity, this is a charming, naturally posed picture of a woman carrying out a familiar, everyday task and is redolent of Edgar Degas' work. However, shoes always carry an erotic charge, and the fact that she is taking hers off after a long, hard day could be a rather heavy-handed allusion either to her love life or to her profession.

(above and page 42)

VENUS DE MILO
Unknown artist
Marble
c. 150–100 B.C.

Probably the most famous statue in the world and a byword for female pulchritude, in spite of the lack of arms: the Venus de Milo or de Melos. She is so called because she was found on the Greek island of Melos in 1820. Note the first recognized case of "builder's crack" —the result of wearing either a shawl or a pair of pants slung low over the hips. On Venus it looks positively seductive.

(above and page 43)

**BAIGNEUSE AUX
OISEAUX**
Felix Vallotton (1865–1925)
Oil on canvas
1919

Swiss artist Vallotton was noted for his simplicity of form, sense of abstract design, straightforward technique, and a fondness for monumentality. All these qualities are present in this picture, which is manifestly a tribute to the Venus de Milo—even the arms are held forward, apparently missing, from the viewer's standpoint. Although the work is entitled Bather with Birds, it is very likely that the subject is meant to be Venus, or Aphrodite, since birds are one of the goddess' particular attributes.

(above and page 44)
L'ODALISQUE
François Boucher (1703–70)
Oil on canvas
18th century

Boucher had a great penchant for female nudity and a matching facility for making the most delicious and playfully erotic pictures featuring the irresistible combination of soft flesh and the swish and purr of silk and velvet. He was particularly fond of the female bottom, which he painted as many times as he could. Compare his voluptuous odalisque, sprawled invitingly on her cushions, with Ingres' cold beauty (see page 113) and consider which one is likely to be more fun.

(above and page 45)
LOVERS
Kitagawa Utamaro
(1753–1806)
Color woodblock print
c. 1788

This is an illustration from the Japanese "Poem of the Pillow," part of the tradition of shunga, or erotic albums or scrolls. Revealed in full, the erotic force of this print comes from what is hidden, rather than what is shown. Utamaro was a celebrated artist of erotic prints and created several albums depicting the sexual act from every angle. However, he preferred the oblique approach; even in the midst of abandoned copulation, the lovers preserve a certain decorum. The emphasis is on the patterns and folds in the fabric of their clothes.

(above and page 46)
HERMAPHRODITE
Unknown artist
Marble
2nd century B.C.

Hermaphroditus was the son of Hermes and Aphrodite. A handsome youth, he attracted the attention of the naiad Salmacis, but refused her advances. One day he took a bath in her spring and she pulled him deep into her pool and asked the gods to unite them forever. Their bodies were joined together as one —an hermaphrodite with female curves and breasts and male genitals. This statue was found broken in the ruins of the Baths of Diocletian in Rome and restored to its former glory. The bed and pillow were added by the great seventeenth-century sculptor Bernini.

(above and page 47)
NUDE MODEL
RECLINING
William Etty (1787–1849)
Oil on millboard
19th century

In Victorian England, Etty was almost a one-man factory for nudes. He painted mostly women, and was inspired by Peter Paul Rubens (1577–1640); his handling of texture was outstanding. There is no indication that this model had any narrative significance, or was even known; however, Etty usually preferred to keep to the Classics, painting Greek (and occasionally Roman) goddesses and nymphs.

(above and pages 48–49)
THE THREE GRACES
Edward Burne-Jones (1833–98)
Chalk on paper
19th century

This is another take on the Three Graces, a perennial favorite with artists since the Renaissance. The accepted composition of the trio is now almost a cliché, but each generation adds its own spin to the classic. In Burne-Jones' version, Beauty, Gentleness, and Friendship display all the drooping charm and skinny wistfulness that characterized the women painted by the Pre-Raphaelites.

(above and page 50)
TWO NUDES WITH
A JUG
August Macke (1887–1914)
Watercolor on paper
1911

Macke was one of the founders of the Blaue Reiter (Blue Rider) group of Expressionist painters in Germany. His own style was a distillation and simplification of a blend of Fauvism and Cubism. Color was always his strong point. His two nudes with a jug have an almost stained-glass quality, so strong is their outline and so lambent their colors.

(above and page 51)

THE FRUITS OF JEALOUSY
Lucas Cranach the Elder
(1472–1553)
Oil on wood
1535

Nudity is secondary to the strife occurring in this scene, in which an extended family appears to have lost the plot somewhat. Cranach's slender nudes, very attractive to a twenty-first-century eye weaned on fashion magazines, nearly always appear in an incongruous woodland setting, regardless of the narrative or allegory they are enacting.

(above and pages 2, 52)

**LOT AND
HIS DAUGHTERS**
Francesco Furini (1604–46)
(attrib.)
Oil on canvas
17th century

An apprehensive Lot is overwhelmed by his two beautiful and scantily clad daughters. Lot (Abraham's nephew) and two of his daughters escaped the destruction of Sodom and Gomorrah. Believing themselves to be the only human beings left, the daughters decided that they must repopulate the Earth, so they plied their father with wine and then seduced him. Each bore a son and so founded the line of Moabites and Ammonites.

(above and page 53)

**THE CREATION OF THE
HIPPOCRENE SPRING
BY A STROKE OF
PEGASUS' HOOF**
Unknown artist
Mosaic
4th century

The mosaic from which this detail comes was discovered in the House of the Nymphs in Nabeul, Tunisia. The artist has managed to render convincing flesh and curves in an unsympathetic medium. Pegasus was the winged horse born from the blood that spilled from Medusa when Perseus beheaded her; his name was connected to the Greek word for a spring of water, and it was believed he created the Hippocrene spring when he stamped his hoof.

(above and page 54)

**WOMAN
DRYING HERSELF**
Edgar Degas (1834–1917)
Pastel
c. 1890–5

A woman is absorbed in drying herself after washing. She appears oblivious to the artist, bending awkwardly to get the towel in the right place. This is one of a series of paintings made by Degas recording the everyday minutiae of women's lives—washing, ironing, hat-making—a subject that had rarely been tackled before. Degas was extremely interested in movement, and in how human muscles performed various actions, which is why he was constantly lured to the ballet and the racecourse.

(above and page 55)

THE THREE BATHERS
Paul Cézanne (1839–1906)
Oil on canvas
c. 1879–82

Another picture from Cézanne on the bathers theme. These massive, solid women seem more like essential parts of the landscape than mobile people. These nudes are not voluptuous: they have a structural resonance. The picture is rigorously composed, with the trees forming a pyramid faintly reminiscent of Mont Ste-Victoire in Provence, Cézanne's other obsession. His reason for returning to the same subjects was to try to refine the image until he isolated the geometry beneath. In this way he was a precursor of abstract art, although he himself was unable to make a painting that did not have an ostensible subject at its heart.

(above and pages 56–57)

THE ROKEBY VENUS
Diego Rodriguez de Silva y
Velázquez (1599–1660)
Oil on canvas
c. 1648–51

This is the only surviving nude painted by the great Spanish artist Velázquez. Sometimes known as The Toilet of Venus, it shows the beautiful, self-absorbed goddess of love preening herself in her mirror, which is held up for her by an obliging putto. It is not typical of Velázquez's work, and it so outraged one woman suffragist that she slashed it as it hung in London's National Gallery in 1914.

(above and page 58)

SISTINE CHAPEL CEILING

Michelangelo Buonarotti
(1475–1564)
Fresco
1508–12

A detail from Michelangelo's great work in the Sistine Chapel in Rome, commissioned by Pope Julius II (1443–1513). Although depicting divine subjects, Michelangelo's concentration on the human form and his Ignudi—beautiful nude youths, as representations of the perfect human form—are what speak to the modern observer.

(above and page 59)

ADAM AND EVE

Henry Fuseli (Johann Heinrich Füssli, 1741–1825)
Aquatint
18th–19th century

A tender image of Adam and Eve discovering themselves, each other, and their sexuality. A gushing spring to the left of the couple signals the outcome of this mutual fascination. In the white slice of sky, diaphanous angels appear to beat their wings in vain, to warn the oblivious couple. This thing is bigger than both of them. Adam seems to have spent a bit too much time at the gym, but perhaps a few weeks of dalliance will soften him up.

(above and page 60)

MALE TORSO

Unknown artist
Marble
c. 1st century B.C.

This is a marble version, made in Rome, of a bronze by the Greek sculptor Polyclitus dating from the fifth century B.C. The statue is of an unknown young man, but what can be seen of the hip-tilted pose may have inspired Michelangelo (1475–1564) when he made his marble sculpture David in 1501–4.

(above right and page 61)

STANDING MALE NUDE

William Etty (1787–1849)
Oil on canvas
19th century

A male nude by the Victorian nude supremo William Etty, who usually preferred to paint women. Etty came from Yorkshire, and it seems very likely that his model, muscled and mature, was a miner.

(below and page 62)

UNTITLED

Tom of Finland (Tuoko Laaksonen, 1920–91)
Drawing
1930s

Read any good books lately? Useful as well as beautiful, the butt-crack of one of Tom of Finland's signature muscular boy-men is used as a book-rest. Tom's avowedly erotic drawings often have an innocent edge, and this image, although dwelling lovingly on the biceps and bulges of the boy heroes, has a domestic atmosphere.

(above and page 63)

BALL GAMES

Unknown artist
Photographic print
1930s

Quels culs! This rather disturbing photograph stars three sets of pert buttocks, the proud assets of young men who know how to achieve strength through joy. The youths are anonymous, and the photograph, taken in the 1930s, is one of a set describing wholesome sports for young persons; nevertheless, it has an ominous atmosphere.

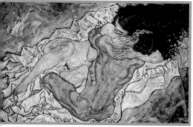

(above and pages 64–65)

THE EMBRACE

Egon Schiele (1890–1918)

Oil on canvas

1917

An embrace between lovers by Egon Schiele. The sheets are rumpled, the lovers are rumpled, we are witnessing postcoital bliss here. Most of the work by Schiele (who died when he was only twenty-eight) was explicitly erotic and he made a specialty of nudes (single, couples, or groups) locked in disturbingly erotic poses. Contemporaries considered his work outrageous, and he was briefly imprisoned in 1912 after being charged with disseminating indecent drawings. Although he died young, time has recognized the importance of his genius.

(below left and page 66)

HERCULES AND ANTAEUS

Hans Baldung Grien

(c. 1476–1545)

Oil on pine wood

1530

Baldung Grien worked in Albrecht Dürer's studio, concentrating on religious painting. He also illustrated mythological subjects, but, however ancient, they were always set in a northern forest. This picture shows Hercules defeating the giant Antaeus by lifting him off the ground and squeezing; Antaeus, son of Poseidon, had so far won every fight he had undertaken because he replenished his strength every time he stood on Earth.

(above and page 67)

BATTLE OF THE GODS

Unknown artist

Marble

c. 180 B.C.

A fragment from the Altar of Zeus in Pergamon showing the Battle of the Gods. Zeus is fighting Porphyrion and two youthful Titans. This huge battle took place between the old order (Titans and Titanesses) and the new order (represented by the massed gods of Mount Olympus under Zeus). After 100 years of struggle, the Olympians won and the Titans were locked away in the innermost chamber of Hades.

(above and page 68)

VENUS AND ADONIS

Titian (Tiziano Vecellio, c. 1488–1576)

Oil on canvas

16th century

Displaying the smooth sweep of her back and the pert curve of her buttocks to great advantage, Venus, the goddess of love, tries to hold back her lover, the beautiful Adonis, from the hunt; he is destined to be killed by wild boars. His death so upsets the goddess that she creates the red anemone flower, which grows where each drop of his blood falls on the ground.

(below and page 69)

THE BATHERS

Jean-Léon Gérôme

(1824–1904)

Oil on canvas

19th–20th century

These bathers are safely fixed in an Oriental bath-house, not discovered in a landscape. Gérôme was the

antithesis of Impressionism, and all his work was meticulously painted and highly finished. Do not look for spontaneity, but be assured that all the detail is spot-on. Gérôme spent a lot of time in the Middle East in general and in Egypt in particular, and most of his paintings have a sort of Eastern penumbra overlaying them. It is the Oriental context that lends the erotic edge to his work.

(above and page 70)

NUDE STUDY

Edgar Degas (1834–1917)

Pastel on paper

19th–20th century

Another intimate nude from Degas; the eroticism of this painting comes from the element of voyeurism. The woman is washing herself, oblivious to the viewer's presence, and Degas is interested mainly in the technical detail of muscle and position. This cool approach yields an unexpectedly hot image. Degas was very interested in developments in photography that were happening at the same time as he was painting, and he often used a camera to provide inspiration or reference. This picture may be the result of working in the studio with a photograph to follow.

(above and page 71)

WOMAN BATHING
Pierre-Auguste Renoir
(1841–1919)
Oil on canvas
19th–20th century

A very magnanimous *derrière* from Renoir in this curious picture. The bather appears to be nose-to-nose with a landscape picture, or to have been thrust into a landscape that is out of synch with what she is doing. Renoir is reputed to have painted on the spot —that is, on location—but this work seems studio-bound.

(below and pages 72–73)

LIFE STUDY OF THE FEMALE FIGURE
William Edward Frost
(1810–77)
Oil on canvas
1842

A surprisingly modern-looking nude by a British artist who was awarded gold medals by the Royal Academy and whose pictures, mostly of mythological subjects, were admired —and on occasions purchased—by Queen Victoria. Only the model's hairstyle gives any clue to the period. Perhaps it is the unadorned background that contributes to the contemporary feel. The sketch is labeled Number 13, so Frost was evidently meticulous in his preparation for major works.

(above and pages 74–75)

BUTTOCKS AND TORSO OF A NUDE WOMAN
Karen Tweedy-Holmes
(b. 1942)
Photographic print
1990

The exclusion of the head, arms, and legs from this image, together with the unusual pose, transforms a nude figure into an abstract study of planes, volumes, and echoing curves. Humanity is drained from the image, but what is left is imbued with the cool sensuality of a marble statue, so that it becomes almost impossible not to want to run your hand over the swell of the buttocks.

(above and page 76)

THE LITTLE FISHERMAN
Pierre Puvis de Chavannes
(1824–98)
Oil on canvas
1881

The androgynous figure with a butt to die for, contemplating his modest catch, was an extremely popular picture in its time. Puvis de Chavannes was a leading Symbolist painter and his work was imbued with a limpid, soulful quality. He is best known for his decorative work, in which he created creditable Italian-style "frescoes" using oil paint and a very light-toned palette. Buildings that he worked on include the Pantheon in Paris and the Public Library in Boston, which was the scene of The Inspiring Muses (1893–5).

(above right and page 77)

THE JUDGEMENT OF PARIS
Joachim Wtewael (1566–1638)
Oak wood panel
1615

The elegant women arranged in distorted poses are the goddesses Athena, Aphrodite, and Hera. Paris is the lucky man judging who is the fairest of them all. Aphrodite wins the golden apple. Athena's contemptuous hand-on-hip pose shows just how well the decision has gone down.

(above and page 78)

NUDE
Amedeo Modigliani
(1884–1920)
Oil on canvas
20th century

A lanky, world-weary nude sprawls on velvet sheets, favoring the viewer with a postcoital gaze. Much influenced by thirteenth-century Italian art, Modigliani painted many nudes, all of whom exuded an unforced, easy eroticism. He painted them so well because they formed such a large part of his life. Handsome and excitingly dissolute, he had many lovers and drank himself to an early death.

121

(above and page 79)

**THE DANCE OF
THE CYMBALISTES**
Frederic, Lord Leighton
(1830–96)
Oil on canvas
19th century

The posturing figure is reminiscent
of Elizabethan miniatures, but the
picture is curiously unerotic. Lord
Leighton, a pillar of Victorian society,
painted many nude figures (paying
great attention to their drapes), but
kept them in a rigid mythological or
classical context. Queen Victoria bought
his first Royal Academy picture.

(above and page 80)

**BATHERS IN
A LANDSCAPE**
Paul Cézanne (1839–1906)
Lithograph
1890–1900

Cézanne returns to his obsession
with bathers and fitting them into
the landscape. This time the models
appear altogether more youthful
and less monumental than the
subjects in other essays. Note the
leaning tree, a leitmotif in the
composition of Cézanne's bathing
pictures. The artist is famous for
working "live"—that is, outdoors,
in the landscape—but it seems
unlikely that he could have bribed
so many members of the Provençal
peasantry to pose in the outdoor
chill for so long: the picture must
have been done in a studio.

(above and page 81)

**YOUNG JAPANESE
NEWLYWEDS IN A BATH**
Horace Bristol (d. 1997)
Photographic print
c. 1946–56

A tenderly erotic view of married
bliss, as the Japanese honeymooners
take their ease in the bath-house of
a ryokan, or traditional inn. The combination of water, steam, glass, and
sexual chemistry makes the simple
composition tingle with excitement.
Bristol belonged to the 1930s' San
Francisco circle that included Ansel
Adams (1902–84) and Edward
Weston (1886–1958) and was one
of the first staff photographers for
Life magazine. After the war he lived
in Japan, but destroyed much of his
work after his wife's suicide.

(above and page 82)

STATUE OF VENUS
Unknown artist
Gilded ivory
2nd century B.C.

A female torso, thought to be Venus,
from ancient Rome. From the position of the legs it looks as if she
might have been running some-
where; the full, fecund buttocks, the
focus of the composition, indicate
fertility and ripeness. Perhaps it is not
Venus, but Proserpina, daughter of
the earth goddess Ceres, trying in
vain to escape from Dis, king of the
underworld, who kidnapped her.

(below and page 83)

NUDE STUDY
Watson (19th century)
Photographic print
1856

The nude figure made an easy
transition from the canvas to the
camera. Photography came into its
own in 1839, with the invention of
the daguerrotype. A quarter of a
century later it had become an art
form, but at this stage one that
borrowed heavily from painting
for its composition and lighting.
Exploitation of the capabilities of
the medium would not begin until
the late twentieth century.

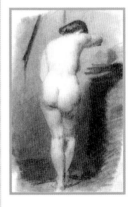

(above and page 84)

**STANDING NUDE
SEEN FROM THE BACK**
Thomas Eakins (1844–1916)
Charcoal and crayon on paper
c. 1903–6

Eakins, possibly the greatest
American artist of the nineteenth
century, was a stickler for realism
and a master of light effects.
Rational and free from affectation,
he used Eadweard Muybridge's
photographs in his lectures, and a
wax figure to check his own work
against. His candor and realistic
attitude were not universally appre-
ciated; in 1886 he was dismissed
from his post at the Pennsylvania
Academy for allowing mixed classes
to work from the nude model.

(above and page 85)

**SALMACIS AND
HERMAPHRODITUS**
Bartholomeus Spranger
(1546–1611)
Oil on canvas
c. 1581

Salmacis and her generous dimpled flanks dominate the composition of this picture by Antwerp artist Spranger. The naiad has her eye firmly fixed on the beautiful youth Hermaphroditus, lurking apprehensively in the background on the banks of her spring. Salmacis is truly, madly, deeply in love with him, and this will be the undoing of them both, as she drags him down into the water and they are literally fused together as one being.

(below and page 86)

MODEL ON HER BREAK
Lovis Corinth (1858–1925)
Oil on canvas
1909

The artist's model ostensibly takes a break from holding an arduous pose; she stretches her arms and rolls her head and neck to release the accumulated tension. She is no longer representing a classical goddess or nymph, but is herself, in the real world, standing between the heap of her clothes and the huge studio stove. The irony is, of course, that she is still posing. Corinth's debt to Impressionism can clearly be seen in the picture's composition.

(above and page 87)

**FEMALE NUDE
PICKING FLOWERS**
Pierre-Auguste Renoir
(1841–1919)
Oil on canvas
19th–20th century

A monumental (some might say lumbering) nude dominates this picture. Once again, a figure painted in the studio is transposed to an outdoor background. It is not clear why she is naked, especially since her rose-plucking companions are dressed, but in this context she has the air of an earth goddess—of an aspect of Gaia or Demeter, come not so much to pick the flowers as to check on their progress. The rosy flush on her shapely flanks echoes the color of the flowers.

(above and page 88)

ORPHEUS
Il Padovanino (Alessandro
Varotari, 1588–1648)
Oil on canvas
17th century

Il Padovanino (the "Padua Kid") specialized in mythological and religious subjects. Here, the Thracian poet Orpheus, star of many classical paintings, plays his anachronistic lira da braccio to soothe the savage beasts: predators and prey together, oblivious of their natural roles. Well-formed Orpheus was a devotee of Dionysus and the lust object of the Maenads, who tore him to pieces after he left them for Eurydice.

(below and page 89)

BAPTISM OF CHRIST
Cornelis van Haarlem
(Cornelis Cornelisz,
1562–1638)
Oil on canvas
1588

A disparate group appears to be observing the baptism of Christ, taking place in the middle distance. The artist, one of three leading Mannerists from The Netherlands, is more interested in the muscled, sculptural shape of the dominant element in his composition, a back view of an anonymous, athletic figure. He is carefully observed, right down to the dirt on his feet. Cornelis founded the Academy of Haarlem and was a great influence on Franz Hals (c. 1580–1666).

**MILO OF CROTONA
DEVOURED BY A LION**
(above and page 90)
Pierre Puget (1620–94)
Marble
1671–82

The agony of the unfortunate Milo is captured in stone in the most famous work by the French sculptor Puget. It was accepted for the gardens at the palace of Versailles, but his distinctive style, which was influenced by Michelangelo (1475–1564) and the Italian Baroque, was not thought suitable for indoor décor. Puget took the rejection hard, perhaps feeling some of the pain experienced by his famous Milo.

(above and page 91)
MILTON: A POEM
William Blake (1757–1827)
Engraving
1804

A title-page illustration taken from Milton: A Poem in Two Books, To Justify the Ways of God to Men (1803–8). Blake's perfectly proportioned man appears to be waiting at the doorway of the poem for this very justification.

(below and page 92)
CHARON TAKES SHADOWS ACROSS THE WATER
Pierre Subleyras (1699–1749)
Oil on canvas
c. 1735–40

Charon the ferryman takes dead souls across the Styx River to Hades, a crossing from which there is no return. The son of Darkness (Erebos) and Night (Nyx), Charon is usually shown as a curmudgeonly old man, demanding payment for his services. In the hands of French history painter Subleyras, he becomes a well-muscled hunk who appears to be much too healthy, alive, and athletic for this dead-end job. Perhaps he is an apprentice on work experience.

(above and page 93)
WARRIOR FROM RIACE WITH HEADBAND
Unknown artist
Bronze
c. 430 B.C.

This bronze was found in the sea at Riace, Calabria, in Italy, in 1972. It is thought to be a votive statue from the sanctuary at Delphi and might have been made by Phidias (d. c. 432), the foremost sculptor of classical Greece. The poser's stance, relaxed and yet ready to go, indicates he was probably a professional fighter.

(above and page 94)
HERCULES RESCUES DEIANEIRA FROM THE CENTAUR EURYTION
Hans Rottenhammer
(1564–1625) (attrib.)
Oil on copper
16th–17th century

In this hectic, crowded scene, Hercules—standing heroically in the center—rescues his wife Deianeira from the clutches of the centaur Eurytion, whom he kills. Centaurs had a reputation for being brutish, lascivious, and easily influenced by wine. This was Eurytion's second attempted abduction and rape.

(above and page 95)
HERCULES, DEIANEIRA, AND THE DEAD CENTAUR NESSUS
Bartholomeus Spranger
(1546–1611)
Oil on canvas
1580s

More trouble with centaurs… Here, Hercules rescues Deianeira from the centaur Nessus, who was carrying her across the raging Euenus River, but tried to rape her on the way. Hercules killed Nessus with a poisoned arrow, but as he lay dying Nessus told Deianeira to take and keep some of his blood, and to smear it onto Hercules' tunic if she ever suspected he had ceased to love her. Some time later Hercules died horribly, unable to tear off his poisoned clothes.

(above and page 96)
THE BATTLE OF THE TEN NUDES
Antonio Pollaiuolo (1432/3–98)
Engraving
c. 1470–5

This early work by Pollaiuolo is his only surviving engraving and reflects his interest in the human figure in movement. As a fight scene it is ludicrous, but as a study in the various ways in which the body can move it is arresting. Pollaiuolo was an avid follower of science in art and dissected many bodies to see how muscles work. His engraving was seen as a study aid by his contemporaries, and copies of it appeared in many a Renaissance studio.

(above and page 97)

**A STATUE BESIDE
THE CANOPUS OF
HADRIAN'S VILLA**
Unknown artist
Marble
1st century A.D.

This statue of a fully armed but naked warrior comes from Hadrian's Villa at Tivoli, Italy—a palatial complex that was finished in A.D. 124. Hadrian (76–138), who was emperor of Rome from A.D. 117, was a renowned soldier, administrator, and lover of the arts. The statue stands by the emperor's canopus, presumably as an eternal praetorian guard.

(above and page 98)

**STUDY FOR
A SCULPTURE**
John Nava (b. 1947)
Oil on canvas
1994

The beautifully illuminated model turns her back on us, allowing the viewer to concentrate on the beauty of the female torso seen from behind. The negative space around the model gives the painting a three-dimensional, sculptural effect typical of Nava, whose work focuses on realistic portraits, nudes, and still lives.

(above and page 99)

LESBIAN LOVERS
Katsushika Hokusai
(1760–1849)
Color woodblock print
1821

A detail from a shunga print by the master printmaker Hokusai, featuring characteristic languid poses and beautiful fabrics. It was made a decade or so after the golden age of Japanese printmaking. Shunga prints were invariably erotic in tone and subject matter, and to avoid punishment from the censor, the artist's signature and the publisher's identifying marks were left off.

(above right and page 100)

**STUDY OF A MALE NUDE
FROM BEHIND**
Tintoretto
(Jacopo Robusti, 1518–94)
Charcoal on paper
c. 1577

After Titian (c. 1488–1576), Tintoretto shares the honors with Veronese (c. 1528–88) as top Venetian painter; indeed, he became the official painter for the Republic of Venice. Titian may have influenced his palette, but Michelangelo (1475–1564) guided his drawing, as can be seen from this heroic male nude, made in the style of the master of Rome. The nude is probably a study for one of the many large-scale decorative paintings for which Tintoretto became justly famous.

(below and page 101)

THE FOUR WITCHES
Albrecht Dürer (1471–1528)
Engraving
1497

In an obvious reference to the many famous renditions of the Three Graces (see pages 113, 117, and 127), an established genre is subverted by painter and printmaker Dürer, who added a fourth "Grace" and branded the quartet as witches, although they have few witchy attributes. The composition and tonal quality are very reminiscent of a painting; Dürer was the first artist to use the medium of engraving almost exclusively to express his undoubted genius.

(above and pages 102–103)

WHAM!
Frank Romero (b. 1941)
Oil on paper
1993

Wham is apparently the name of the model, although this bold brace of buttocks might equally allude to the painting Whaam! by Roy Lichtenstein (b. 1923), which shows a fighter plane blowing up. Romero uses the technique of sgraffito to pull out the yellow image from beneath the purple overpainting, in a manner suggesting the first impression received when a sheet is pulled off a nude figure. A California native, Romero was a founder of Los Four, the group that galvanized Hispanic artists. His work is typified by richly colored canvases, painted sculptures, and neon-enhanced images of California, particularly Los Angeles.

(above and page 104)

THE RAPE OF
THE DAUGHTERS
OF LEUKIPPOS
Peter Paul Rubens (1577–1640)
Oil on canvas
c. 1618

The heavenly twins Castor and Pollux scrum down on Hilaria and Phoebe, daughters of their uncle Leukippos, to remove them from their official fiancés, another pair of cousins, Idas and Lynceus. The abduction results in marriage and motherhood for Hilaria and Phoebe, but discord and death for the four young men. Rubens brings his customary verve of excecution to an already lively scene.

(above and page 105)

DANAË
Giovanni Battista Tiepolo
(1696–1770)
Oil on canvas
1736

A very languid Danaë, in dire need of exercise after a long time imprisoned in her bronze tower, is visited by Zeus in the form of a shower of gold coins. Tiepolo is better known as the last great fresco painter, but also made genre paintings in which his taste for the grandiloquent remained unmoderated. Rubens was a great influence, as Danaë's monumental thighs show.

(above and page 106)

ANGELS AND DOVES
François Boucher (1703–70)
Oil on canvas
18th century

In biblical terms, angels are awesome spiritual beings, graded in nine ranks. The second rank comprises cherubim, symbols of heavenly light and knowledge. In early art they were represented as grave young persons, but by the eighteenth century they had been sentimentalized and had become lesser figures, tumbling about rococo canvases as chubby, rosy-cheeked infants. Boucher has them playing with doves, symbols of peace.

(above right and page 107)

CORNUCOPIA
Jacob Jordaens (1593–1678)
Oil on canvas
1649

The almost indefatigable Hercules wades into action once more; this time killing the river god Achelous in order to win Deianeira from him. During this struggle the god's horn is broken off, and a group of strapping nymphs and naiads turn it into a cornucopia: the horn of plenty that never empties. The Flemish artist Jordaens, a success in his own right, often assisted Rubens, but his style is much earthier than the flesh-meister's, with even chunkier bodies, a darker palette, the paint troweled onto the canvas, and composition that pays greater respect to the law of gravity.

(below and page 108)

VENUS OF WILLENDORF
Unknown artist
Sandstone and red chalk
c. 20,000 B.C.

This votive figure, only 4in./10.5cm. long, was found at Willendorf in Austria. It offers a remarkable instance of foreshortening in a three-dimensional figure. It is thought to be a fertillty token, perhaps offered to ensure a good harvest or safe childbirth. Some argue that such figures were made by women themselves; others that the figurines were little bits of portable porn made by men and carried on long, lonely hunting expeditions.

(above and page 109)

THE BATHERS
Gustave Courbet (1819–77)
Oil on canvas
1853

A detail from a painting that unites many of Courbet's themes: realism, sensuality, and the everyday rendered in epic terms. The central bather is no nymph but a real woman trudging back to the daily grind after a refreshing bathe. Courbet's realistic approach was castigated for "deliberately seeking ugliness." He was a kind of prototype of the late-nineteenth-century artist: dashing, romantic, policitally engaged, opinionated, unconventional, stroppy, antiauthoritarian, and passionate about his own vision of reality.

leave artists much creative scope, Rubens went for the creation of the flesh. Baroque grandeur and amplitude were his forte, and although the taste for this kind of image is currently out of favor, nobody does it better than Rubens.

(below and page 128)
NUDE
Imogen Cunningham
(1883–1976)
Gelatin silver print
1932

(above and pages 110–111)
THE THREE GRACES
Peter Paul Rubens (1577–1640)
Oil on canvas
c. 1636–40

Probably the most famous group of beautiful women painted by probably the most famous painter of female pulchritude. What could be better than a fetching Rubens derrière? Three fetching derrières, that's what. As the established composition of this genre favorite (see pages 113 and 117) did not

American artist Imogen Cunningham worked as a photographer from 1901 and, after focusing initially on romantic photographs and then plant studies, she turned to portraiture in the mid-1930s. She was a founder member of the group known as f/64, together with Ansel Adams (1902–84) and Edward Weston (1886–1958). This luscious nude is very reminiscent of Weston's work and "reads," visually, as an organic composition rather than as a sexual proposition.

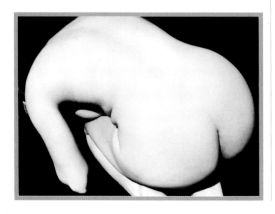

picture credits

AKG, LONDON 16–17 / Berlin, Pergamon Museum 67 / Bucharest, State Museum of Art 18 / Copenhagen, State Art Museum 107 / Dresden, Gemäldegalrie, Alte Mesiter 21, 86 / Graz, Private Collection 20 / Eric Lessing: Mainz, Mittelrheinisches Landesmuseum 50; Paris, Musée du Louvre 42, 44, 46, 89, 92; Reggio Calabria, Museo Nazionale 93; Vienna, Kunsthistorisches Museum 19, 85, 94, 95, 108; Vienna, Österreichische Galerie in Belvedere 64–5 / Madrid, Museo del Prado 88 / Giles Mermet: Tunisia, Nabeul Museum 53 / Moscow, Pushkin Museum 51 / Munich, Alte Pinakothek 104 / Paris, Musée du Louvre 22–3 / Private Collection 43 / Stockholm, University Collection 105 / Warsaw, Nawdowe Museum 66

THE BRIDGEMAN ART LIBRARY: Ashmolean Museum, Oxford, UK 47 / Birmingham Museums & Art Gallery, UK 48–9 / Bonham, London, UK, Private Collection 60 / British Museum, London, UK 59 / Chester Beatty Library, Dublin, Irish Republic 24 / Christie's Images, London, UK 70 / Gabinetto dei Disegni e Stampe, Uffizi, Florence, Italy 34/ Giraudon: Musée du Petit Palais, Paris, France 55 / Hermitage, St Petersburg, Russia 100 / Lauros-Giraudon, Louvre, Paris, France 25, Musée d'Orsay, Paris, France 35 / Leamington Spa Museum and Art Gallery, Warwickshire, UK 32 / Ali Meyer, Kunsthistorisches Museum, Vienna, Austria 14 / Musée Fabre, Montpellier, France 109 / National Gallery, London, UK 56–7 / National Gallery of Scotland, Edinburgh, Scotland 30, 54 / Philadelphia Museum of Art, Pennsylvania, PA, USA 40 / Phillips, The Fine Art Auctioneers, UK 37 / Prado, Madrid, Spain 15, 2 and 52, 68, 106, 110–11 / Private Collection 33, 76, 96, 99 / The Stapleton Collection, UK 6 and 12 / Tel-Aviv Museum, Israel 71 / Towneley Hall Art Gallery and Museum, Burnley, Lancashire, UK 61 / Victoria & Albert Museum, London, UK 45, 72–3 / Whitford & Hughes, London, UK 41, 69 / Peter Willi: Musée Girodet, Montargis, France 36; Private Collection 87

CORBIS: Horace Bristol 81 / E. O. Hoppé 27 / Hulton Deutsch Collection 83 / Mimmo Jodice 82 / National Gallery Collection 77 / Philadelphia Museum of Art 84 / Karen Tweedy-Holmes 74–5 / Werner Forman 97 / The Brett Weston Archive 28–9

IMOGEN CUNNINGHAM TRUST 128

DAVID HOCKNEY 10–11, 31

HULTON GETTY 63

LIZARDI/HARP, Pasadena, California: William Fogg 13 / E.K. Kitchen 26 / Steven Lungley 5, 38–9 / John Nava 98 / Frank Romero 102–3

SUPERSTOCK 79, 80 / Huntington Library, San Marino 91 / Italian Barnes Foundation 78 / Louvre, Paris 90

THE TOM OF FINLAND FOUNDATION 62

Front cover: AKG, London / Eric Lessing: Musée du Louvre, Paris.

Every effort has been made to trace all copyright holders and obtain permissions. The publishers sincerely apologize for any inadvertent errors or omissions and will be happy to correct them in future editions.

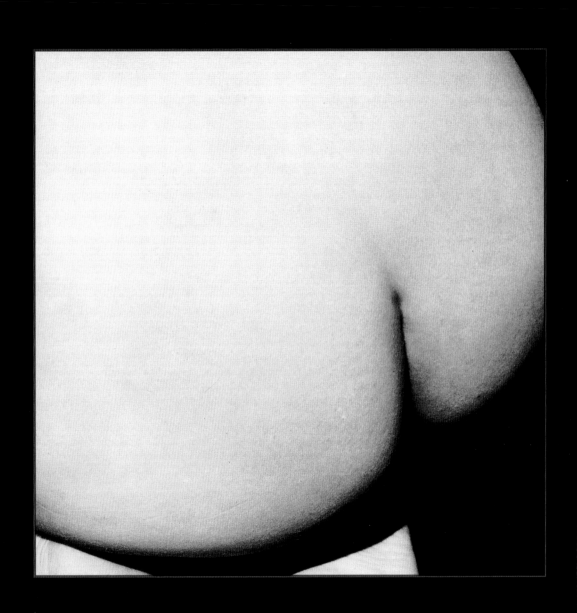

the end